JOURNAL FOR THE STUDY OF THE OLD TESTAMENT
SUPPLEMENT SERIES
69

Editors
David J A Clines
Philip R Davies

BIBLE AND LITERATURE SERIES
16

General Editor
David M. Gunn

Assistant General Editor
Danna Nolan Fewell

Consultant Editors
Elizabeth Struthers Malbon
James G. Williams

Almond Press
Sheffield

ZEPHANIAH

A Prophetic Drama

Paul R. House

The Almond Press · 1988

Bible and Literature Series, 16

General Editor: David M. Gunn
(Columbia Theological Seminary, Decatur, Georgia)
Assistant General Editor: Danna Nolan Fewell
(Perkins School of Theology, Dallas, Texas)
Consultant Editors: Elizabeth Struthers Malbon
(Virginia Polytechnic Institute & State University, Blacksburg, Virginia)
James G. Williams
(Syracuse University, Syracuse, New York)

Copyright © 1988 Sheffield Academic Press

Published by Almond Press
Editorial direction: David M. Gunn
Columbia Theological Seminary
P.O. Box 520, Decatur
GA 30031, U.S.A.
Almond Press is an imprint of
Sheffield Academic Press Ltd
The University of Sheffield
343 Fulwood Road
Sheffield S10 3BP
England

Typeset by Sheffield Academic Press
and
printed in Great Britain
by Billing & Sons Ltd
Worcester

British Library Cataloguing in Publication Data

House, Paul R.
Zephaniah, a prophetic drama.
1. Bible, O.T. Zephaniah—Commentaries
I. Title   II. Series
III. Series
224'.9607

ISSN 0260-4493
ISSN 0309-0787

ISBN 1-85075-075-0

CONTENTS

ACKNOWLEDGMENTS

Several people deserve my gratitude for their contributions to this project. In its first life the manuscript served as a doctoral dissertation. My thesis advisor Dr John D.W. Watts encouraged me to write a literary analysis of biblical prophecy and offered many valuable suggestions about format and methodology.

Two men helped shape the book into its present form. James G. Williams noted various places where revisions and additions were needed. I am also thankful to Dr Williams for recommending the manuscript to Almond Press. David Gunn, the editor of this series, was especially helpful with comments on the content of Chapter 2. His willingness to work with me and his enthusiasm for the project will always be appreciated.

My colleagues at Taylor University were supportive of this publication. Dr Richard J. Stanislaw, Academic Dean at Taylor, provided funding for part of the typing of the manuscript. Mrs Sharon Gray and Mrs Rita Koch typed portions of the text, and Sharon even read every word she typed! The members of the Religion Department were extremely encouraging, though some may doubt the importance of Zephaniah or literary analysis.

Most of all I thank my family for their help. My parents and my wife's parents have lent moral and financial support. My wife Becky typed some of this project's first draft and has always supported my professional endeavors. Our daughter Molly provides comic relief and a general sense of joy to our lives. To these two special people the book is dedicated.

For each kindness I am grateful.

Paul R. House
Upland, Indiana

To Becky and Molly

Chapter 1

INTRODUCTION

Unlike some of the minor prophets, Zephaniah has received minimal critical attention. A perusal of books and articles on this Old Testament book takes relatively little time. Even those who write about Zephaniah sometimes have small regard for its uniqueness. Note the words of Frank Eakin, who says 'Thus we recognise that there was little that was new in the message of Zephaniah. Primarily he built upon the prophetic mentality developed before his time' (275). Brevard Childs describes the prophecy as a mere compendium of other prophetic views (460). John M.P. Smith, in the International Critical Commentary, offers some praise of Zephaniah, but finds him inferior to other prophets. According to Smith:

> Zephaniah can hardly be considered great as a poet. He does not rank with Isaiah, nor even with Hosea in this particular. He has no great imaginative powers; no deep insight into the human heart is reflected in his utterances; nor any keen sensitiveness to the beauties of nature. His harp is not attuned to the finer harmonies of life like that of Jeremiah. He had an imperative message to deliver and proceeded in the most direct and forceful way to discharge his responsibility. What he lacked in grace and charm, he in some measure atoned for by the vigour and clarity of his speech. He realized the approaching terror so keenly that he was able to present it vividly and convincingly to his hearers. No prophet has made the picture of the day of Yahweh more real (176).

Other writers echo similar sentiments about the book.

Are such assessments of Zephaniah adequate? Granted, Zephaniah participates in a rich tradition of prophetic thought, but surely more can be said for the book. While past and present scholarship tends to dismiss the prophecy after brief study, such an appraisal of the book is unsatisfactory for several reasons. First, scholars tend to judge

Zephaniah without doing in-depth research into its content. Second, Zephaniah is lightly regarded because it has been examined almost solely through historical-critical methods which are patently unable to deal with a prophecy like Zephaniah that has few known historical facts behind it. Historical critics have divided the book into pericopae, judged the historicity of the pericopae, and argued over the date of the pericopae. Never have the historical critics understood the overall fabric of Zephaniah. Third, scholars dismiss Zephaniah out of a lack of proper appreciation for the book as canonical scripture. That is, the prophecy is treated as if it is superfluous to the Old Testament message as a whole. A survey of how Zephaniah has been interpreted will reveal these tendencies.

The History of Zephaniah Interpretation

The great reformers Luther and Calvin began an emphasis on a historical analysis of Zephaniah that has dominated the prophecy's interpretation for over 400 years. Both men had philological and expositional concerns, but the foundation of their studies was history. Luther is careful to describe Zephaniah's date and purpose in his commentary. Concerning the date he says:

> He prophesied before the time of the Babylonian captivity. The title verse of the prophet indicated this when he says that he prophesied 'in the days of Josiah, the son of Amon, king of Judah'. You see, under Zedekiah, who was surrogate for the sons of Josiah, the entire nation was carried off into Babylon (318).

Most of Luther's comments hinge on his understanding of Zephaniah's pre-exilic status. Concerning the book's purpose Luther declares:

> His goal is like that of all the prophets: the kingdom of Judah was going to be destroyed by Chaldeans; those of the tribe of Judah who still survived were going to be led into captivity; yet, some trace of Judah would be revived and saved for the sake of Christ (318).

The coming 'day of the Lord' is explained, primarily, as the Babylonian captivity (320).

While Luther sets the purpose of and general time period for Zephaniah, Calvin discusses the issue of when during Josiah's reign the prophet preached. Calvin believes that even after Josiah's reforms the people refused to serve Yahweh. He writes:

It is hence an obvious conclusion, that the people had ever been
wedded to impiety . . . though they apparently pretended to worship
God, and, in order to please the king, embraced the worship
divinely prescribed in their law; yet the event proved that it was a
mere act of dissimulation, yea, of perfidy (186).

Thus Calvin concludes that Zephaniah preached after Josiah's
reform, or after 621 BCE.

It is important to note Luther's and Calvin's opinion on Zephaniah
because they set an agenda for interpretation that has continued.
Their discussions focus on author, situation, and date in Josiah's
reign. Scholars may disagree with Luther and Calvin, but they follow
their agenda with few additions.

During the last century a number of able historical commentators
discussed the book. C.F. Keil, S.R. Driver, and H. Ferguson, from
different theological positions, reflect the practice of exploring
Zephaniah's date, setting, lineage, and theology. Keil and Ferguson
basically agree with Luther and Calvin. They note that the virtually
unknown prophet Zephaniah authored the book, that the Babylonian
threat forms the prophecy's situation, and offer a post-Josianic
reform date for the book (Ferguson: 42-43; Keil: 117-21).

S.R. Driver, in his greatly influential *An Introduction to the
Literature of the Old Testament*, discusses a new topic in Zephaniah
studies. Following in the wake of Wellhausen, Driver shows that
certain passages in Zephaniah may not be 'authentic', or date from
the prophet himself (342). Source critics generally denied that 3.14-
20 was originally in the book, and questioned other portions as well
(342). Driver himself, always the mediator, states:

> Only 2.11 seems to be really out of place. 3.14-20 may be more
> doubtful: its buoyant tone forms a marked contrast to the sombre,
> quiet strain of 3.11-13, and the period of Israel's judgment seems to
> be past (cf. v. 15a). Still, the picture is, of course, an imaginative
> one; and the question remains whether it is sufficiently clear that it
> was beyond the power of Zephaniah's imagination to construct it
> (342-43).

Driver's work effectively surveys the tendency of late nineteenth-
century scholars to divide Zephaniah into 'authentic' and 'non-
authentic' oracles. The goal of these writers is clearly to discover the
date of each phrase of the text. In their zeal for historical accuracy,
however, these writers failed to realize that the unity of Zephaniah is

broken by this compartmentalizing of the text. Without the 'non-authentic' passages the fluidity of the book suffers.

Early twentieth-century historical critics were similar to their predecessors in their source-critical findings. The commentaries of John M.P. Smith and George Adam Smith represent the academically excellent but repetitive works of that time. Issues of the past are handled with great expertise, yet the results are much the same. Both writers, like Driver, state that 3.14-20 is an addition to Zephaniah's authentic oracles (J.M.P. Smith: 173; G.A. Smith: 38-39). John M.P. Smith calls 2.8-11, 15 and 3.6-13 secondary as well (173).

One area in which both scholars differ with earlier writers is Zephaniah's date. Both men cite the Scythian invasion of Egypt as the inspiration for Zephaniah's doom oracles, and therefore date the book before Josiah's reform. John M.P. Smith asserts:

> The occasion of Zephaniah's appearance as a prophet seems to have lain in some imminent danger to his nation. He evidently regarded the day of Yahweh as close at hand (1.7). In accordance with the character of earlier prophecy in general and of the day of Yahweh prophecies in particular, it is probable that Zephaniah interpreted the approach of some foreign army as heralding the dawn of Yahweh's day. The event that best meets the requirements of the situation is the Scythian invasion (169).

G.A. Smith basically agrees with this position. He dates Zephaniah in 625 (40), and John Smith dates the book about 627 (170).

Even with this slight shift of date the issues of Zephaniah interpretation are not radically altered. Foreign threat and moral decadence are still the major elements of the prophecy's situation, the 'day of Yahweh' remains the major theme, and Josiah's reform is still the date on which the book's origin hinges. It must also be noted that the inadequacies of earlier works still remain. The text of Zephaniah is still broken into pieces with little regard for its overall artistry. The attempt to date the text tends to fragment the text itself.

More recent historical-critical works offer various ways of approaching Zephaniah without reaching new conclusions. Arvid Kapelrud's monograph holds Zephaniah's creative ability in high regard and delineates Zephaniah's text, structure, and theology. Kapelrud offers a great number of word studies, and generally tries to illuminate the text by linguistic means. He calls his method of interpretation a 'morphological approach', and defines it as a mixture of form criticism and sociological analysis (10). The results of this method, however, differ little from earlier historical and linguistic commentaries.

Other scholars examine Zephaniah through linguistic analysis. Liudger Sabottka employs excellent philological tools in his study, including parallel Ugaritic words and phrases, and although he furthers the etymological understanding of Zephaniah he does not discuss its larger components. Despite a paucity of information in these areas, Gunter Krinetzki explores the composition and layers of redaction in Zephaniah. His conclusions are dubious because they are built on a practically non-existent historical foundation. Hubert Irsigler reverts to examining the book through form-critical methods. Again, while these people are competent historical scholars they are unable to say more about Zephaniah than the writers before them.

A few commentators have focused their efforts on the date of Zephaniah. Louise Pettibone Smith and Ernest R. Lacheman compare Zephaniah to exilic and post-exilic books and date the prophecy deep in post-exilic times.

> The book is almost as definitely pseudepigraphic as Daniel and should, like Daniel, be read against the background of 200 B.C. Luckily the survival of a name (1.1, Zephaniah) in connection with the old oracle (1.4ff.) gave it its place in the Book of the Twelve (141).

Certainly the methodology of Smith and Lacheman is questionable. To compare the language of a book with post-exilic works to find its date is unsatisfactory. Surely as many parallels to pre-exilic scripture exist as to post-exilic works.

Donald Williams also seeks to move Zephaniah's date from its traditional time period. Because of the sacrificial imagery of 1.7ff. and the other cultic overtones in the book Williams declares that Zephaniah was a cultic figure (86). He then equates the prophet Zephaniah with the priest of the same name found in 2 Kings, Jeremiah, and Zechariah (86). Once this identification is made Williams places the ministry of Zephaniah down to the fall of Jerusalem. Zephaniah and Jeremiah are therefore contemporaries. Williams concludes his argument by claiming:

> Thus, in my opinion, in view of the evidence, no good reasons can be given to deny the date of Zephaniah's work in the period following Josiah's death in 609 B.C. and extending to his own death

in 587 B.C. The name Zephaniah in 2 Kings, Jeremiah, and
Zechariah refers to the same man, whose preaching is preserved in
one of the books of the minor prophets (88).

Williams' assertion of a late date ignores the plain intention of the
book's heading, and he has to re-date a number of passages to make
his theory work. The strongest position on Zephaniah's date remains
one during the turbulent days of Josiah's reign.

As has already been stated, little original work has been done on
Zephaniah. Historical studies have produced a picture of Zephaniah's
situation, text, and redaction, and scholars have explored these areas
again and again. Linguistic analyses have been done, but have not
altered the findings of historical critics. It is not unkind to say
Zephaniah study has stagnated. The work has been well done, but it
is finished.

Another difficulty with past interpretations is that they have
tended to particularize the text into pericopae, the pericopae into
words, and words into etymologies. The prophecy has been atomized
without the text being reassembled. Interpreters have lost a sense of
the unified construction of Zephaniah. Mention is made of the
overriding theme of Yahweh's day, and then the atomizing goes on
unabated.

In all fairness it must be said that the book itself does not easily
accommodate historical critique. Smith, Lacheman, and Williams
show what varying ideas can be forwarded about Zephaniah's
identity and career. Zephaniah's *exact* situation is impossible to
obtain, as is evidenced by the centuries-old discussion of whether
Zephaniah writes before or after Josiah's reform. Any redaction or
source analysis of Zephaniah is dubious too. The book offers no hints
at its composition, as does Jeremiah.

New questions arise, however, from the past studies. If no clear
redaction of Zephaniah can be made, then how does the book work as
a unified construction? If the day of Yahweh is the main theme, how
is that theme developed in the book? If no extensive description of
Zephaniah exists, how is the prophet portrayed in Zephaniah? If the
text is not to be atomized, how does the action proceed through the
whole book? Other questions arise from these, such as: 'What is
Zephaniah's genre?' and 'What role does dialogue between Yahweh
and the prophet play in the prophecy?' Thus, one must build on
historical studies and move on to other problems instead of dealing
continually with old questions.

Methodology

If historical criticism is no longer used, then some new method of approaching Zephaniah must be sought. In recent years many scholars have turned to various forms of literary criticism to explicate the Old Testament. Long before, however, scholars led primarily by Richard G. Moulton surveyed the Bible as literature. In collective and individual works he discusses the Bible's literary nature, genres, characters, plots, and themes. His most important work is *The Literary Study of the Bible*, in which he presents a methodology for examining each section of the Bible as literature. No major biblical scholars followed Moulton, however, so literary criticism was ignored for years.

Form critics deal with elements of the text such as genre, poetics, and imagery, but always with the decidedly historical interest of finding the text's *Sitz im Leben*. Form criticism therefore has a distinctly historical emphasis. It also tends to relate better to small sections than to large blocks of material.

In 1969 James Muilenburg published a lecture entitled 'Form Criticism and Beyond' in which he urges exegetes to go beyond form-critical analysis to rhetorical criticism. Muilenburg explains the purpose of rhetorical criticism as follows:

> And this leads me to formulate a canon which should be obvious to
> us all: a responsible and proper articulation of the words in their
> linguistic patterns and in their precise formulations will reveal to
> us the texture and fabric of the writer's thought, not only what it is
> that he thinks, but as he thinks it (7).

To achieve this purpose rhetorical critics explore verbal structures, grammar, meter, word play, and strophes. Rhetorical critics define the boundaries of a passage and then analyze it paragraph by paragraph, sentence by sentence, word by word, and syllable by syllable. Obviously it is a linguistic analysis. It normally does not deal with larger concerns such as genre, themes, plot, or characters.

Somewhat similar to rhetorical criticism is structuralism. While used in departments of literature for many years, structuralism has only recently been introduced in biblical studies. David Robertson notes that the first major presupposition of structuralism is that 'appearances are not reality' (549). Reality is explained by truths hidden below the surface. These truths are called 'deep structures'. The second important presupposition is that 'deep structures express themselves as codes' (549). Codes, voiced by language, explain the deeper meaning of reality. Structuralists, like rhetorical critics, break a text down into its smallest units. Robertson concludes:

> The entire model should be compared to the analysis of language into phonemes, morphemes, words, phrases, sentences, etc. Structuralist criticism may begin at any one of these levels, but it finally always proceeds from whole to ever larger whole (549).

Thus, the structuralists divide pericopae into phonetic, grammatical, and structural units to show how the overall text holds together.

Structuralism also deals with plots and characters. Plot is discussed by showing how each object and subject relate to one another. Characters are defined by whether they are acting or acted upon. Actions of the characters are charted to show how often a character approaches a certain object. Speeches are analyzed for deeper meanings. Mixing linguistics and psychology causes structuralism to be an overly esoteric discipline.

Reader response critics stress the importance of highlighting the reader in the interpretative process. Rather than placing ultimate importance on the text, as historical, rhetorical, and structuralist critics do, reader response advocates claim their 'goal is no longer a meaning *behind* the text which creates distance but rather a meaning *in front of* the text which demands involvement' (McKnight, 1985: xviii). This 'in front of' meaning is different to every reader. Thus, all meanings are subjective, but are somewhat regulated by social and aesthetic conventions. As McKnight observes:

> When the external circumstances are altered or when particularly strong individuals influence the literary tradition, the cultural atmosphere may change and concretizations will assume a visibly different form (36).

Most reader response analyses break down a text like structuralist studies, search for as many levels of meaning as possible, and apply current trends of thought to each meaning. Readers are encouraged to consider how the literature has impact on their own lives. Pleasure or utility can be goals of this process.

Partly because it employs structuralist techniques to examine a text reader response criticism is also an overly obscure method of literary analysis. Language is 'deconstructed' to its smallest components to find interpretative possibilities, which fragments the text. The fragmented literary piece can only be put together by subjective redesign. Less value is placed on the text itself. In the study of the Bible the importance of the text must be stressed or the reader's understanding will not attain the level the literature itself intends. As holy scripture the Bible transcends the individual reader, though it does invite study and analysis. Because *the text* 'has life' the reader's world is enlivened.

Robert Alter makes a significant contribution to literary analysis of the Old Testament in his monographs *The Art of Biblical Narrative* and *The Art of Biblical Poetry*. Alter argues for the validity of literary study of scripture and uses literary criticism to explicate biblical narrative and poetry. Alter defines literary analysis by writing:

> By literary analysis I mean the manifold varieties of minutely discriminating attention to the artful use of language, to the shifting play of ideas, conventions, tone, sound, imagery, syntax, narrative viewpoint, compositional units, and much else; the kind of disciplined attention, in other words, which through a whole spectrum of critical approaches has illuminated, for example, the poetry of Dante, the plays of Shakespeare, the novels of Tolstoy (1981: 12-13).

The author defends the use of literary methods of interpretation in biblical studies by noting that scripture has all the features of literary works—plots, characters, verse, etc. He also asserts that literary criticism is at least as constructive as historical criticism (1981: 21).

In his analysis of biblical narratives Alter treats the materials as prose fiction. That is, the biblical stories exhibit all the characteristics of other works of fiction. Fiction is not a pejorative term to Alter, since it means the Bible has the best of both historical and mythological content (1981:27). Because he believes the Bible contains prose fiction, Alter discusses the point of view, plot techniques, characterization, conventions, and dialogue of various narratives. This methodology embraces the larger components of these stories in a way rhetorical criticism and structuralism, because of their emphasis on linguistics, cannot. A discussion of Alter's views on Old Testament poetry is included in Chapter 2.

Northrop Frye has long been interested in the literature of the Bible. His chapter on genre in *Anatomy of Criticism* includes a lengthy discussion of the Bible as an 'encyclopaedic' art form (315-26). By encyclopaedic Frye means that the Bible contains a great number of genres. *The Great Code: The Bible and Literature*, however, is Frye's most extensive work on biblical literature. This work is based on archetypal criticism, which seeks mythical motifs or patterns in literature. Such motifs as creation, promise, and kingdom are traced throughout the Bible (171). Opposing archetypal figures such as God and Satan, angels and demons, sheep and wolves, paradise and hell, and bride and whore are noted (166-67). Through this methodology Frye seeks to show that the Bible is a unified work. In fact, he calls the Bible 'the most systematically constructed sacred book in the world' (1967:315). Certainly Frye's chief contribution to biblical studies is this insistence that the Bible is thematically and archetypically a literary whole.

Besides charting trends in literary criticism, David Robertson has written his own study of Old Testament literary criticism, *The Old Testament and the Literary Critic*. Robertson chooses a comparative approach to the Old Testament. He places Psalm 90 alongside Shelley's 'Hymn to Intellectual Beauty' to show the poetic elements they share (55-70), and relates Exodus 1-15 to the Bacchae (16-32). The strength of this method is that genre study is advanced through the comparing of biblical passages with similar kinds of literature.

Robertson's book has several problems. The chief of these difficulties is his insistence that if the Bible is literature then it cannot be scripture.

> However, and here is the rub, the Bible as literature is fiction. Its dramatic personae are imitations of real people, its actions imitations of real actions, and its thoughts imitations of real thoughts. . . . Therefore, its power as literature is hardly what its power as scripture is (84).

Such a false dichotomy between literature and scripture is unnecessary. Studying the literary nature of the Bible no more negates the binding nature of the Bible as holy scripture than does examining its historical components.

Most, if not all, of these methodologies have come from secular literary criticism. Indeed Moulton, Frye, and Alter have published works on American and English literature. It is natural, then, to note secular literary methods helpful to the interpretation of Zephaniah.

One such method is genre criticism. Traditionally, critics have examined literary works to establish what *kind* of literature they are. Since Aristotle's *Poetics*, the genres (kinds) of drama, lyric, and epic have been studied. The presence of the novel, short story, etc. have added a fourth genre, prose narrative, to the older three.

Genre studies in literary criticism have changed in the past several decades. Formerly it was held that individual genres contain certain features and that those features never overlap. More recent works have concluded, however, that similarities exist between genres. Enough similarities have been uncovered that scholars like Austin Warren and Rene Wellek question the value of any genre criticism (219ff.). One must realize, though, that whatever likenesses exist between, for example, Trollope's *Barchester Towers* and Eliot's 'The Waste Land', they are not enough to obscure the differences between the two. Likewise in Old Testament studies it is clear that Ruth and Psalm 23 vary in kind. Genres do interact with one another, but there is still great value in generic study. The importance of genre analysis is evident when one realizes that

> This first 'what are we dealing with?' step is highly necessary, since different literary genres are judged according to different standards. We do not expect, for example, the sweep and grandeur of an epic in a love lyric, nor do we expect the degree of detail in a short story that we find in a novel (Guerin:11).

Many other approaches identified with secular literary criticism could be discussed, such as psychological analysis, sociological analysis, and moralistic analysis, but the approach most helpful for biblical studies is formalistic criticism. Formalism in the United States is most often associated with the rise of the 'New Criticism' in the 1930s and 1940s. John Crowe Ransom, Cleanth Brooks, Allen Tate, and Robert Penn Warren are the most famous practitioners of formalism. All were critics who sought to read 'art for art's sake' instead of reading out of an interest in historical or psychological background. Wilbur Scott correctly observes:

> Without question, the most influential critical method of our time is the formalistic. It has commanded the zeal of most of our leading critics . . . is, in fact, the method one almost automatically thinks of when speaking of contemporaty criticism (179).

While Scott's remarks are over twenty years old, they still reflect the importance of formalism in literary criticism.

Formalistic analysis attempts to analyze the components of a text to uncover its meaning. Wilfred Guerin defines formalism by noting:

As its name suggests, the object of 'formalistic' criticism is to find
the key to the structure and meaning of the literary work—a key
that inevitably reveals itself as necessary to the experience of the
work as an art *form* (45).

To find this key one must pay 'attention to *what* the literary work
says, and to do that, we must first consider *how* it is said' (47).
Formalistic criticism is not concerned with the historical background
of a literary work, the psyche of the author, or the archetypes in the
literature. Rather, formalists treat the text *as it is*, believing it has
'life' in and of itself. Close readings are vital in formalism. A text is
studied to reveal themes, motifs, and messages (what it says), and to
uncover plot, characterization, setting, and imagery (how it says). To
summarize: a literary work is a structure of words, means in a precise
way, and is understood from within rather than without. Thus, form
and content work together to give a text meaning.

It is impossible to employ all aspects of all the methodologies
mentioned above. Nor would it be appropriate if it were possible. It is
both possible and appropriate, though, to use the most pertinent
aspects of these models as a methodology for reading Zephaniah.

From the methodologies surveyed two necessary presuppositions
arise. The initial one is that the text itself is valuable aside from its
historical background. The art form itself has intrinsic value. A
passage's meaning must come from the text and move out rather
than *vice versa*. A second presupposition is that the text is a unity. An
interpreter must find and explain the common threads of a literary
work. Rather than viewing Zephaniah as a *collection* of disparate
pericopae, it must be seen as an artistic whole. Both presuppositions
argue for the fundamental value of the text in interpretation.

With these presuppositions understood it is possible to present the
methodology and arrangement of this book. A wedding of genre
criticism and formalism is attempted. Genre theory and close
reading form the nucleus of the work.

Since Zephaniah's genre is the major factor in its literary
character, the second chapter chooses and explores a proper theory
of genre. Broad methods of literary expression are examined first,
with emphasis placed on prose and poetry. Section two narrows the
focus to the major genres of literature, sub-genres built from major
genres, and modes of expressing genres and sub-genres. Drama is
highlighted in the discussion in order to demonstrate Zephaniah's
prophetic drama later in the book. Through this process a sound
genre theory will arise and be used throughout the work.

Chapter 3 examines the literary elements of Zephaniah to gather data that reveal the book's genre. Several aspects of the prophecy are included in this analysis, including words and phrases, themes, point of view, characters and characterization, mood, plot, dialogue, time, and imagery. In short, the results of a close reading of Zephaniah are presented. These parts of the book are discussed so that the overall picture of Zephaniah will be clearer. Each section of the chapter is, quite obviously, vital to the discovery of the genre of any work of literature. Genre theory is established in Chapter 2, and Chapter 3 offers the materials that make that theory usable.

Having presented the theory and data, it is necessary to bring the two together. Chapter 4 unites theory and close reading to uncover Zephaniah's genre. Section one seeks to compare the prophecy with aspects of the major genres. Once the comparison is made its dramatic nature becomes more obvious. Since Zephaniah is drama, then, section two demonstrates in a much fuller way how the literary characteristics of the book fit the dramatic genre. In section three all comparisons cease and the book is presented as it is: prophetic drama. Zephaniah's dramatic nature is therefore seen as the best explanation for the book as a whole.

Chapter 5 offers a translation of Zephaniah and explains the significance of interpreting Zephaniah as prophetic drama. A translation is made to provide a proper text for the drama and to demonstrate how the text is divided in its dramatic form. Chapter 5 therefore serves as a summary by putting the text in the form discovered in the research and by expressing the value of the project's conclusions.

Zephaniah definitely deserves more attention than it has received. Almost always relegated to the status of second-class prophecy, the book has been generally unappreciated. Perhaps this approach to Zephaniah opens new avenues of study. No doubt some historical critics may challenge the conclusions of this project. Given the paucity of advancement in Zephaniah studies, however, nothing can be lost by this approach—and much can be gained. The fact is, Zephaniah thinks, moves, and means as drama. It can excite the reader as drama. In short, perhaps Zephaniah *can* rise from the ashes of scholarly neglect.

Chapter 2

A BRIEF SURVEY OF GENRE CRITICISM

Genre criticism has existed since the time of Plato and Aristotle. These fourth-century BCE philosophers identify three basic genres and create areas of discussion about them. Plato locates three types of narrators in literature: one who speaks for himself, one who has one or more characters speak for him, and one who mixes the two (16-17). Heather Dubrow identifies these three as

> Dithyrambic poetry, which was generally a form of ode in which the poet was accomplished instrumentally, is cited as an example of the first type; tragedy and comedy represent the second; the epic is an instance of the third or mixed form, as the poet intersperses dialogue in his own narration (47).

Thus, Plato describes lyric poetry (ode), drama (tragedy and comedy), and epic. Each imitates life in its own way (16-17).

While Plato's work is important, Aristotle's *Poetics* is the most discussed ancient comment on genre. In fact, all generic studies since Aristotle reflect his ideas in some way. Aristotle sets forth his generic methodology when he says:

> I propose to treat of Poetry in itself and of its various kinds, noting the essential quality of each; to inquire into the number and nature of the parts of which a poem is composed; and similarly into whatever else falls within the same inquiry (31).

His emphases on the 'kinds' of poetry, the 'qualities' of poetry, and the 'plot' of poetry are the heart of all genre criticism. Aristotle also offers three kinds of literature for discussion: Lyric, Epic, and Drama (31). He shows how each genre imitates life (32), imitates characters (35, 44), and uses plot (36-44). He further declares Tragedy the highest of the arts (55). Few other aspects of genre could be discussed. It is important to state at this point that Aristotle understands the fluidity of the generic forms. He sets few boundaries for the genres that cannot be crossed.

Medieval writers note the presence of genres, but, as Dubrow observes, 'they generally devote what little attention they do bestow on style to rhetorical devices' (54). At no time, though, is the importance of generic distinctions denied. One area of genre study that receives attention is the genres of the Bible. O.B. Hardison explains:

> When the ancient tradition was assimilated by the Christian authors, comparisons were drawn between Latin and Hebrew authors. Jerome was fond of such comparisons. 'David' he remarked, 'is our Simonides, our Pindar, our Horace', and it is to Jerome that Latin tradition owes its conception of Job as a tragedy, Pentateuch as a heroic poem, and Ecclesiastes as an elegy. Bede . . . takes the same approach. Job to him is an heroic poem, while Deuteronomy and Psalms 118 and 119 are elegies. The Song of Songs is a biblical drama; Ecclesiastes is the biblical equivalent of the 'narrative' form illustrated in antiquity by the *Georgics* and the *De Rerum Nativia*; and Job is an example of the 'mixed' form used by Homer in the *Iliad* and Vergil in the *Aeneid* (Preminger, Hardison, Kerrane:11).

The medieval scholars did not just look for epic, lyric, and drama. Instead they offer 'theories for a number of modes not included in the Greek and Latin rhetoric manuals, notably the prophetic' (Dubrow: 12). This interest in biblical genre is a precedent for placing scripture in literary categories.

During the Renaissance genre analysis became a pervasive force in literary criticism. In fact, it may have reached its most influential status at that time. Because copies of primary texts like Aristotle's *Poetics* became readily available for the first time there was much interest in genre study. More recent works were compared to Aristotle's standards to see if they met classical 'qualifications' to be true epic, drama, or lyric. Rosalie Colie notes the existence of 'bitter critical battles in sixteenth-century Italy over Dante's *Commedia*, Speroni's un-Sophoclean tragedy *Canace e Macareo*, Ariosto's and Tasso's epics, and Guarim's tragicomical play' (2). Renaissance critics think that new works should conform to the classical style. According to Colie:

> generation after generation of Renaissance young men were willing to turn to antiquity, adapting to their needs and desires those

elements in antiquity which they could recognize as useful or symbolically relevant (3).

Through this emphasis on the past a prescriptive element entered genre studies. Scholars claim 'a high style befits its high subject-epic or tragic; a low style a low-subject, comedy or some lyric forms' (Colie:3). Styles are not to be mixed lest 'pure' genres disappear (Colie:3). Much of the opposition to genre criticism comes from rebellion against such prescriptions. Many great works *do not* follow a set of rules, it is argued, and a creative artist must be free to write as he or she pleases. Although Renaissance scholars greatly further genre analysis through their reverence for Aristotle, they place strictures on literature Aristotle himself would not have liked.

Seventeenth- and eighteenth-century critics also hold generic studies in high esteem. So great is their reverence for Aristotelian theory that the era is called the 'Neoclassical' age. Pope, Dryden, and Johnson are among the best of the neoclassical writers. These thinkers seek to describe genres and how they are composed.

Their stress on classicism is evident since the 'typical schematism for at least the major poetic kinds, such as drama and epic, came ultimately, though with many modifications, from the *Poetics*' (Crane:377). Great care was taken to discuss genre in all literary analyses. R.S. Crane observes:

> The systematic statement of an art, however, was seldom considered complete without a section, usually a long one, on its various kinds; and here again the richness of the terminology bequeathed to the neoclassical critics by their predecessors in antiquity and the Renaissance for whom the question of genres was a central question of art, coupled with the possibility of obtaining criteria for definition and classification not only from distinctions of artistic matter and means but from differences in the natural faculties of artists and audiences, permitted a mode of analysis that was often (as in Boileau and Dryden) elaborate and subtle to a degree (377).

In this era, then, genre analysis is the starting place for further critical comments. Comments on author, audience, and text follow discussions of genre.

The neoclassical period also produced writers who stress the individuality of each literary piece. W.R. Keast notes that Samuel Johnson believes author and audience are the most important aspects of literature, rather than the form the literature assumes (399).

Johnson also claims each author changes a genre by adding a new work to that genre (Keast:396). These ideas help balance genre study. An author's individuality and an audience's response must not be lost in the study of form, since artistry includes both form and creativity.

Neoclassicism was strongly rejected by Romanticism in the early nineteenth century. Romantics stress feeling, common language, spontaneity, and pleasure in poetry instead of form. This insistence on creativity and imitation of spoken language led the Romantics to reject rigid genre analysis. Wordsworth divorced his poetry from Neoclassicism by asserting:

> There will also be found in these volumes little of what is usually called poetic diction; as much pains has been taken to avoid it as is ordinarily taken to produce it; this has been done ... to bring my language near to the language of men, and further, because the pleasure which I have proposed to myself to impart is of a kind very different from that which is supposed by many persons to be the proper object of poetry (302).

Likewise, Coleridge rejects generic distinctions with statements like 'a poem contains the same elements as a prose composition' (336). William Hazlitt also denounces the content and conclusions of Neoclassicism (405).

Romanticism's reaction against genre criticism is particularly significant because of its lasting influence. Negative comments on genre analysis have continued in a similar vein. While their dislike of genre goes too far, the Romantics offer the same cautions as Samuel Johnson. Individual thought and creativity must not be neglected in literary criticism.

Twentieth-century attitudes about genre criticism reflect the contrasting beliefs of Neoclassicism and Romanticism. Distrust of generic distinctions is prominent in the writings of Benedetto Croce and scholars who follow him. Croce argues that genre study is philosophically indefensible and a contributor to poor writing. Concerning the former idea he writes:

> a classification of intuition-expressions is certainly permissible, but is not philosophical: individual expressive facts are so many individuals, not one of which is interchangeable with another, save in its common quality of expression (67-68).

Concerning his other argument Croce claims:

> It is needless to say how much harm has been done by rhetorical distinctions. Rhetoric has often been declaimed against, but although there has been rebellion against its consequences, its principles have, at the same time, been carefully preserved (perhaps in order to show proof of philosophical consistency). In literature the rhetorical categories have contributed, if not to make dominant, at least to justify theoretically, that particular kind of *bad writing* which is called *fine writing* according to rhetoric (69).

In his discussion of writing according to rhetorical conventions Croce sounds much like Wordsworth. A more scathing condemnation of genre criticism is hardly possible.

American formalists (New Critics) also neglect detailed genre analyses. They believe each work exists as a significant entity regardless of how it relates to other literature. Ironically, though, formalism offers many of the best tools to explore genre. By delineating a text's *form* and substance formalist critics show how different texts relate to the shape and style of other works. Thus, through close readings formalism carefully reveals the characteristics of literary pieces, and genre study is a short step away from this process.

While the romantic convictions about genre are still alive, many scholars follow the neoclassical impulse to study literary forms. In the United States the 'Chicago School' of critics, so named because most of the scholars taught at the University of Chicago, has argued for the validity of generic distinctions. R.S. Crane, Elder Olson, and W.R. Keast, among others, are the chief thinkers of this school. They comment on forms identified by Aristotle and some neglected by him. Russian formalism and structuralism also address generic issues. Perhaps the most significant individual proponent of genre over the past three decades is Northrop Frye. Frye seeks to categorize the types and sub-types of epic, lyric, drama, and prose (1967:243-337). His insistence on the importance of genre is justified, for studying the forms of literature helps bring order to literary criticism. Alastair Fowler and Joseph Strelka are two more contemporary critics who stress genre.

Reader response critics also deem genre distinctions important. Mary Gerhart studies four scholars, E.D. Hirsch, Hans-Georg Gadamer, Tzvetan Todorov, and Paul Ricoeur, and concludes each finds generic distinctions significant. Hirsch is the most 'radical' of the four, since he claims there is no meaning in a text without genre

(313). A text's genre is thus the key to its meaning. Gadamer thinks a reader can only interpret a text as its historical background is understood, which, in turn, is discovered only when genre is taken into account (314-15). Todorov finds that genre analysis helps the reader find a work's structure, thus aiding the organization of interpretation (315). Finally, Ricœur declares that mastering genres teaches readers an overall critical competence and lets them see the need to have the text change their lives (316-17).

All four critics demonstrate the validity of genre criticism. Genre studies not only illuminate a text, these scholars claim, they also illuminate a reader. Good interpretation is dependent on understanding what a text is historically and structurally. Without this realization the reader's response is impoverished.

What, then, can be said about the value of genre? Certainly the ancient, medieval, renaissance, neoclassical, and modern writers who stress genre analysis do so for good reasons. The most important of these reasons is that generic studies reveal what a text is so what a text says can be heard. As C.S. Lewis claims:

> The first qualification for judging any piece of workmanship from a corkscrew to a cathedral is to know *what* it is—what it was intended to do and how it is meant to be used. . . The first thing is to understand the object before you: as long as you think the corkscrew was meant for opening tins or the cathedral for entertaining tourists you can say nothing to the purpose about them (1).

It is therefore impossible for critics to discard completely the notion of genre. Form and content both supply a text's meaning. Not even those who distrust the results of genre criticism can neglect it completely.[1]

On the other hand, the romantics, Croce, *et al* are right to say the presence of form does not stifle the originality of a work. The author is still free to shape the work as he or she pleases. What these critics fail to see is that many authors, especially Milton and Spenser, are at their best when creating new stories to fit ancient patterns. In short, genre studies are still valid, with the cautions that authors are unique and that genres are heterogenous instead of monolithic.

In modern times several attempts to describe biblical genres have been made. Like their medieval predecessors, these attempts focus mainly on the fact that the Bible contains many genres. Form critics locate many types of poems in the Old Testament, including hymns, laments, and doom oracles. These scholars deal carefully with texts, and then compare passages to create categories of poems. All this work is done, however, with the intention of discovering the passage's historical *Sitz im Leben*. Northrop Frye calls the Bible's genre 'encyclopaedic' since it contains most, if not all, of the major genres (1967:315). A host of recent writers deal with the aspects of Old Testament narratives. Richard G. Moulton attempts to create new names for biblical genres. He discusses, besides lyric, epic, and drama, such forms as the doom song, rhapsody, symbolic prophecy, and dramatic prophecy (363ff.). Moulton believes these forms have comparative roots in the three classical genres.

Even with such genre studies, the analysis of biblical genre is certainly an undeveloped area. There is a great need for a coherent methodology for doing genre criticism both of long and short works. In the prophetic literature there is a special need for genre study, since there is a large prophetic corpus. If the prophetic genres can be explicated then the canonical emphases of the prophets can become clearer.

Broad Expressions of Genre:
Prose and Poetry

Genre studies deal with specific and general expressions of literature. General expression is the linguistic medium of a literary piece. In other words, does the author write prose or poetry? Specific expressions require the most discussion. These expressions include whether a piece is drama, lyric, or epic. Both general and specific expressions of Zephaniah need to be discussed to form a comprehensive approach for deciding its genre.

As a prelude to more detailed genre discussions and a close reading of Zephaniah it is necessary to decide whether the book is prose or poetry. While some scholars may doubt the necessity of this approach, it is a process that is logical for interpretation, since learning the difference between prose and poetry aids the understanding of syntax, images, and metaphors.

Prose
The more typical of the two language forms, prose composes perhaps as much as two-thirds of the Old Testament. Prose generally follows the syntactical pattern of verb-noun-object, and even when it varies

for emphasis it normally returns to its typical pattern. Hebrew prose is governed mainly by the use of perfect and imperfect verbs. The addition of *waw* consecutive to imperfect verbs allows sentences to flow from one sequence to another ('and then'). Relative pronouns are dotted throughout prose to clarify the passage's context. Thus, the translator of prose is seldom bothered by eccentric variations in sentence structure.

Prose is an action-oriented medium. It describes events and the implications of those events. Very seldom will prose convey abstract meaning or reveal the inner reflections of a character. Books with a consistent narrative purpose, like Samuel and Kings, are best served by prose, since they attempt to disclose specific deeds and events.

As could be expected from its syntactical characteristics, prose is linear in aim. That is, its story line will usually move from a fixed starting point to a definite conclusion. Whether the life of an individual, tribe, or nation is described, prose includes a beginning, middle, and end. Commentary on why the action proceeded as it did is often included, but is always based on the action itself. Prose is therefore objective in purpose and best suited to story. Prose narrative is in no way simplistic, as Robert Alter has conclusively shown. Each story has unique elements that make it creative and artistic.

Poetry

Poetry plays an undeniably important role in the composition of the Old Testament. Each of the three traditional divisions of the canon contain poetry. Most significant for this study is the predominance of prophetic poetry. Norman Gottwald writes:

> Lamentation, Obadiah, Micah, Nahum, Habakkuk, and Zephaniah are poetic in their entirety (with the exception of superscriptions). The greater parts of Job, Isaiah, Hosea, Joel, and Amos are poetic, and Jeremiah is about one half poetry (829).

As Gottwald says, Zephaniah is poetic except for its inscription. This judgment is perhaps the most universally shared aspect of Zephaniah studies. This realization necessitates a study of ancient Hebrew verse.

Unlike prose, Hebrew poetry utilizes a number of syntactical schemes. Verbs, nouns, participles, or infinitives may regulate the action of a phrase. Relative pronouns are used sparingly. Any student of Hebrew trained on prose faces a new world when translating poetry.

Poetry is also reflective and circular in nature. Objective presentation of a linear event often gives way to subjective statements about feelings and events. For example, 2 Kings 24-25 describes the Babylonian conquest of Judah but Psalm 137 relates the poet's feelings about captivity. While prose is linear, poetry revolves around the reflection of the composer. Either the poetry remains the poet's thoughts or expands beyond the poet and then comes back to the poet's opinion (e.g. Zeph. 1.10-13). In this way poetry is a circular process that returns to its initiator.

Hebrew poetry differs from the poetry of Western culture. There is little rhyme in Hebrew poetry, and stanzaic or strophic patterns are hard to discern. Its meter rarely follows an obvious pattern, which sets it apart from traditional Greek, Roman, Italian, and English poetry. Old Testament poetry does have its own rhythm, though, and makes full use of imagery, metaphor, word play, and other poetic devices.

The rhythm of Old Testament poetry is shaped through thought and sense patterns. Robert Lowth was the first scholar to state that these thought patterns are structured in parallel sequences. Gottwald defines 'parallelism' as the process of 'balancing thought against thought, phrase against phrase, word against word' (830-31). Lowth uncovers three categories of parallelism: 'Parallels Synonymous, Parallels Antithetic, and Parallels Synthetic' (xii). Lowth and others point out subdivisions of these three groups, but no one has successfully disproved the existence of parallelism itself. Certainly Lowth errs in assuming *all* Hebrew poetry contains parallelism, and that Hebrew prose has no parallelism, yet its constant presence in Hebrew poems makes parallelism a valid concept. Parallelism appears in Babylonian and Ugaritic texts, thus connecting Hebrew poetry with its cultural neighbors (Lambert:33).

Synonymous parallelism is probably the most recognizable form. It is achieved by a second phrase completing, complementing, or re-stating an initial phrase. In simple forms the phrases are divided by a caesura, or pause, that marks a break in the two separate statements. The phrase can also be distinguished by a simple *waw* conjunction, which begins the second line. In more complex passages an extra line, or idea, may be needed to complete the parallel, or a block of lines may parallel another block of lines. An example of simple

synonymous parallelism is Zeph. 2.4, and a more complex example is
Zeph. 3.1ff.

Antithetic parallelism is an initial thought balanced by an opposite
statement. Antithetic forms are found throughout the Old Testament,
but are especially prevalent in Proverbs where contrasts are often
highlighted. Whether moving from the positive to the negative
(Zeph. 1.13) or the negative to the positive (Prov. 13.4), antithetic
parallels present stark contrasts. Besides for didactic purposes,
antithetic parallels are sometimes used by a prophet to warn or
rebuke (e.g. Jer. 13.16-17 and Zeph. 1.13).

Lowth's final form, synthetic parallelism, is the most nebulous of
the three. Lowth says synthetic parallelism 'consists only in the
similar form of construction' where parallelism is formed by the
'turn of the whole sentence, and of the constructive parts; such as
noun answering noun, verb to verb' (xxi). This category could too
easily become a 'catch all' for any difficult form. Perhaps this
grouping could be better described as cumulative parallelism, since
many passages are parallel in that they pile image upon image (Zeph.
1.14-16). Also, it must be said that much poetry has parallelistic
tendencies but no definite pattern. These sections are parallel in
syntax, subject, and mood more than by similar or conflicting
statements. Zephaniah definitely contains such passages. Certainly
this category points out the subtle nature of much Hebrew poetry.

Recently several writers have attempted to refine traditional
notions of parallelism. James Kugel argues that parallelism is a
process of intensification, or heightening, that fits few if any
discernible patterns. To make his point he cites the differences
between the truly parallel tendencies of Ugaritic poetry and Old
Testament poetry, and offers excellent discussions of the various
kinds of poetic lines in Scripture. Kugel believes the essence of
Hebrew verse is that

> B follows A, and its containing differentiated verbal themes or
> other morphological and syntactic differentiations seems designed
> to draw attention to this circumstance, 'A is so, and what's more,
> B'. The foregoing examples are decisive in the domain of
> morphology and syntax in the same way that sharpness, after-
> wardness, overt subordination, and the like are decisive in
> Semantics (23).

Because of his emphasis on the 'what's more' element of the
second part of phrases Kugel denies that Old Testament poetry is

really parallelistic in Lowthian terms. Rather, the so-called poetic phrase is a linguistic method of clarifying one meaning and moving on to the next more precise meaning (51). No two lines are truly parallel, then, for the second sentence is more precise than the first. New syntactic elements arise that make 'B more than A'.

Kugel's rejection of the common view of parallelism does not mean that he finds no order in Old Testament poetry. In fact, he asserts that there is great artistry both in the shortest line and longest pericope. Kugel notes that the 'emphatic, rhetorical closure . . . was capable of elaboration to increasingly high levels of symmetry and design, and frequently combined with other elevating features' (95). The detailed analyses in *The Idea of Biblical Poetry* demonstrate how intricate and unified Hebrew verse really is. What Kugel concludes is that there is no way to collectively describe the phenomenon of biblical poetry. He summarizes:

> Though biblical poetry and its meter have an honored place in the history of scholarship, it might be wiser to restrict the use of these terms—to speak, in more neutral (and, alas, colorless) language, of biblical Hebrew's 'high' or 'rhetorical' style, and to call the Bible's songs simply songs, its prayers prayers, and speeches speeches (302).

The greatest contribution Kugel makes to poetry studies is his emphasis on Hebrew poetry as a system of gradually more intense and precise statements. Surely he is correct in his assertion that versets do much more than merely parrot one another. Each word, phrase, and sentence has a unique importance that furthers the author's point. Poetry is dynamic, not static.

Other parts of Kugel's work, however, are flawed. To conclude that Lowth's idea of parallelism is mostly invalid is an extreme position that ignores basic Old Testament patterns. Kugel also implies that Lowth finds only sameness in poetry, which is hardly the case. Finally, the failure to see a definite difference between Old Testament prose and poetry is incorrect. One may argue the nature of Hebrew verse, but one can hardly dismiss its existence any easier than one can the poetry of other cultures.

Robert Alter has arrived at some of the same conclusions as Kugel about the 'intensification' element of Hebrew poetry. He disagrees, though, with Kugel's refusal to call versets poetry, and argues that individual lines become more understandable when one admits the existence of biblical poetry. As he claims:

> Once one recognizes that there is a formal system of biblical
> versification distinct from the prose, the nuances of relation
> between parallel formulations come into sharper focus and, equally
> important, it is easier to see the interplay between lines as well as
> the possibilities of relation between the internal structure of the
> line and the structure of the poem (1985:18-19).

Most of the 'interplay between lines' is a 'heightening or intensification
(as in the paradigmatic case of numerals), of focusing, specification,
concretization, even what could be called dramatization' (19).
Intensification occurs through the poet's use of verbs and their
resultant adverbs, nouns and adjectives, and strictly syntactical
modifications (cf. 21-26).

More unique than his survey of intensification is Alter's analysis of
how the poet creates a story line without producing an overt
narrative style. This artistic technique is particularly important in
Zephaniah, where the ramifications of the Day of Yahweh are
displayed without a prosaic method of writing. What results in
prophetic poetry is a kind of verse narrative in which each couplet or
triad leads to the next.

To establish his theory of how poetry moves from line to story
Alter first recognizes the importance of heightening. Even within
individual couplets there is a progression to the next thought
sequence. Next Alter notes how Hebrew poetry develops conse-
quentiality from intensification. Alter believes that at its most basic
level

> narrative movement forward in time is typically generated by the
> establishing of a series of linked actions that, according to the
> poetics of parallelism, are approximate equivalents but prove to be,
> on closer inspection, logically discriminated actions that lead
> imperceptibly from one to the next (39).

In other words, a first step is to apply the principles of line
intensification to the larger poetic pericope. On a more intricate
level, the poet utilizes overlapping verbs and nouns to create verse
narrative. Alter cites the second chapter of Joel as an example of this
process:

> The poet here is less interested in an illusion of seamless temporal
> progression than in a steady, solemn advance—spatially, from the
> distant mountains up to and over the walls of the city and into the
> houses—marked by a mounting drumbeat, and for this the model

of incremental repetition is particularly apt: they run, they dance, they run, they scale a wall, they go; indeed, they go, they swarm, they run, they scale, they come in the windows like thieves (43).

Alter utilizes the best of traditional parallelistic views and refines them in his work. Poetry is still treated as poetry, yet the artistry of how the poet forges a plot line from verse is elucidated. Alter agrees with what is true in Kugel and builds a constructive discussion from traditional elements Kugel dismisses.

Some examples from Zephaniah will help clarify the positions of Kugel and Alter. Intensification is evident in many places, particularly in the opening verses. Note the unfolding clarifications in 1.2-3:

> I will sweep away everything
> > from the face of the earth,
> > > says Yahweh. (general)
>
> (indeed) I will sweep away man and beast.
> (in fact) I will sweep away the birds of the
> heavens and the fish of the seas.
>
> (what's more) I will overthrow the wicked
> > and I will cut off man
> > > from the face of the earth,
> > > > says Yahweh. (much clearer than 1.2)

Yahweh moves from general cosmic to specific personal judgment, with each line clarifying the last.

Zephaniah 3.1-5 shows how Hebrew poetry goes from line to story. Verse one introduces Jerusalem as a rebellious, defiled, and oppressing city. The next four verses progressively describe *how* Jerusalem earned these descriptions. The key to moving the narrative forward in 3.2 and 3.4b is a series of similar verbs, while in 3.3-4a common adjectives provide movement. Verse five displays both methods. Note the progress created by the underlined terms in 3.2-4:

> She *listens* to no voice.
> > She *accepts* no correction.
>
> She *does not trust* in Yahweh.
> > She *does not draw near* to her God.
>
> Her princes within her
> > are *roaring lions*.
>
> Her judges are *evening wolves*
> > who leave nothing for morning.

> Her prophets are *wanton,*
>   *treacherous* men.
> Her priests *profane* the holy.
> They do *violence* to the law.

Often all parts of parallel lines are related, but the verbs or adjectives are usually more compelling. Each couplet moves the story forward through synonymous, complementary, intensifying, or consequential statements.

Poetic devices in the Old Testament are similar to those in other languages. Metaphor, alliteration, and assonance are commonly employed. In Zephaniah, regular metaphors for God (for example) include Yahweh as Priest (1.7-8), Judge (3.5, 8), and King (3.15). Zephaniah 1.17-18, where the *k* sound is so prominent, is a good illustration of alliteration, with the *o's* of 3.1ff. serving as examples of assonance.

Beyond individual metaphors is the creation of an overall metaphorical atmosphere in poetry. As Mary Gerhart and Allan Russell point out, metaphors are ontological and epistemological in nature, for they suggest a distinct way of observing reality. Metaphors shock the reader into seeing truth in a new way by comparing dissimilar objects. As Gerhart and Russell claim:

> The metaphoric act distorts a world of meanings in such a way as to make possible an analogical relationship between one known and another known, an analogical relationship that was not possible before the metaphoric distortion took place (119-20).

Truth is unveiled when a reader makes the connection between these distorted analogues.

In Zephaniah most of the metaphors help create a picture of the day of Yahweh. Cities are compared to sheep pens, human flesh to dust and dung, and Yahweh to a human parent. Each image is calculated to reveal the judgment and mercy of God as they are unfolded on His day. Such juxtaposed ideas jolt the reader's mind into recognizing the gravity of the prophet's declarations. By providing this jolt, the metaphorical world implied in Zephaniah is a chief conveyor of truth. Chapter 3 offers a further discussion on how metaphors function in Zephaniah.

Once a decision is made about the linguistic medium used in a passage the interpreter is able to make better decisions as the close reading is attempted. Certain words, phrases, characters, plots, and ideas will be better understood when seen in a prosaic or poetic context.

Narrow Expressions of Genre:
Genre, Sub-Genre, and Mode

As was shown above, there are a number of ways to study genres. Special problems exist for anyone discussing genre, including how to categorize genres, how to account for the creativity of the author, and how to explain the interrelationship between genres. Alastair Fowler proposes cogent answers to these problems in his *Kinds of Literature*. Fowler says genres are fluid by nature. They have certain basic characteristics but also have elements that grow and change. He observes that 'Genres appear to be much more like families than classes' (42). While noting the fluidity of genres, Fowler firmly believes in the importance of genre study.

> Every work of literature belongs to at least one genre. Indeed, it is sure to have a significant generic element. For genre has quite a different relation to creativity from the one usually supposed, whereby it is little more than a restraint upon spontaneous expression. Rightly understood, it is so far from being a mere curb on expression that it makes the expressiveness of literary works possible. Their relation to the genres they embody is not one of passive membership but of active modulation. Such modulation communicates. And it probably has a communicative value far greater than we can ever be directly aware of (21).

Genres

Fowler's methodology employs three key terms: kind, sub-genre, and mode. The first of these terms indicates that separate genres do exist because different works exhibit distinct features. Artists choose to express themselves through various mediums. It is possible to discover what is characteristic of these mediums even if it is impossible to say what is *always* present in them. Each artist maintains a unique personal style while sharing a common genre. For Fowler, ' "kind" is equivalent to "historical genre", or the unhappily named "fixed genre" ' (56). For the purpose of this study the three classical 'fixed' genres, epic, lyric, and drama, are studied, since these genres are poetic in their ancient forms, as is Zephaniah. Drama is given the most attention because of its importance to the rest of the book. Fowler lists several features that distinguish kinds (genres) of literature.

1. Most kinds have a distinctive *representational aspect*, such as narrative, dramatic, discursive.
2. Every kind is characterized by an external *structure*.
3. In ancient criticism, *metrical structure* was . . . genre linked.
4. As every kind has a formal structure, so it must have a *size*.
5. Closely related to size is *scale*.
6. *Subject* may be limited generically.
7. Closely related are the *values* inherent in all kinds.
8. Each kind has an emotional coloration, which may be called *mood*.
9. Many kinds used to have a characteristic *occasion*, at least initially.
10. Occasion, in its imaginary, attenuated form, coalesces with the stylistic feature *attitude*, which is often characteristic in the short poetic kinds.
11. Narrative kinds may have a distinctive *mise-en-scène*.
12. *Character* is the focus of much existing genre theory.
13. The action of a kind may have a characteristic structure.
14. Every kind has its range of appropriate *style* (56-70).

This list clearly shows how even similar genres have distinct characteristics. When a close reading of a work is completed its generic elements can be seen and its differences from, and affinities with, other literature made plain.[2]

Because of its size and scope, there are fewer examples of epic in world literature than of drama and lyric. Homer is considered the father of epic, and his *The Iliad* and *The Odyssey* are prototypes of later epics. Following Homer, Virgil adapts Greek epic to his Roman audience. Virgil uses Homer's epic structure in *The Aeneid*, but his themes and intentions are different, as will be explained below. While many neoclassical writers attempt to write epics, John Milton is the best crafter of epics in this era. His *Paradise Lost* and *Paradise Regained* capture the form and spirit of Greek and Roman epic.

Several categories of epic have been proposed. Milton suggests two epic forms when he states 'the two poems of Homer and those other two of Virgil and Tasso are a diffuse, and the book of Job a brief model' of epic (126). Apparently a diffuse form is one like *Paradise*

Lost when a full-scale epic is presented, and a brief epic is one like Job or *Paradise Regained* where a lesser amount of characterization, plot, scope, and size are present. C.S. Lewis also proposes two categories of epic: primary and secondary (12). Unlike Milton, who divides epics primarily by size, Lewis believes primary epic is early epic and secondary epic that which grew out of early epic (12). The former type is basically oral, courtly, full of pomp and aristocratic pageantry. Its style is characterized by stock phrases, ritual, realism, focused subject, and a willingness to leave characters and situations unchanged (18-31). Building on these principles, secondary epic moves from the particular to the universal. It takes a single event and makes it happen in a great space of time; it features few people and gives them universal significance; and it treats the past and gives it present importance. The story spreads out in action and time, shows great transitions, includes archetypal patterns, and utilizes an elevated style (32-46). Thus, the 'simple' epics of Homer grow into the more complex epics of Virgil and Milton.

Lewis' two categories work well, and 'are useful as a broad initial division for convenience of description' (Fowler: 161). Homer's epics do deal with singular subjects such as the fall of a great city (*Iliad*) and the return of a great fighter from war (*Odyssey*). They also present limited characterization and a less universal scope. Virgil and Milton build on Homer to chart the founding of an empire (*Aeneid*) and the fall of the human race (*Paradise Lost*). Neither category is superior, but each is a different kind of epic.

Several elements characterize the epic. Aristotle declares that the epic takes a single action for its subject. That single action is unveiled by a clear beginning, middle, and end, and presents a picture of life (50). An epic is narrative in form, is thus able to describe many actions even if they happen simultaneously, and has little or no first-person narration (51). As was stated above, Lewis notes the presence of stock phrases, ritual, elevated style, and universal themes in epic. Certainly the poetry of early epic differs from that of drama and lyric because epics were often recited from memory. Familiar lines (stock phrases) are used to aid the speaker's memory. Characters in epics have various functions. The hero, though human, is larger than life and able to surmount nearly any obstacle. He also has the favor of the gods. The foil to the hero can be either noble or evil, but never has the favor of the gods. Stock characters, good, evil, comic, etc., are present to move the plot and illuminate major characters.

Unless one sees the Bible itself as a great epic, there is no classical epic in scripture. There is certainly no verse epic. Richard G. Moulton claims the absence of verse epic does not negate the presence of prose epic and mixed epics (229-30). Milton's notion of Job as a smaller epic has merit, as does Moulton's emphasis on other kinds of epic. Epic *elements* exist in Job and in other biblical passages even if no clear example of epic appears in scripture.

Just as epic is the longest generic form, so lyric is the shortest. Since lyric is poetic, the statements made in the section on biblical poetry apply here. Lyric is generally considered to be reflective, musical, self-contained, and ornamental (Frye, 1967:245). Lyric has been produced by all the great poets of the centuries, including Pindar, Shakespeare, Milton, etc. Lyric occurs in many parts of the Old Testament, but is of course most prevalent in Psalms. Since the psalms are such good examples of lyric, they will be used to illustrate the characteristics of that genre.

The poet's world is an important element in lyric. Unlike drama and epic narrative where audience and reader are quite essential, lyric is addressed to God, the poet, or a particular individual. As Frye states, 'The poet, so to speak, turns his back on his listeners, though he may speak for them, and though they may repeat some of his words after him' (1967:250). In the psalms, the writer may praise (Ps. 9), or question God (Ps. 10) or remind himself of God's goodness (Ps. 23). The reader is privileged to learn these personal thoughts. These reflections voice the 'I-Thou' relationship of the inner devotions of a follower of Yahweh. If these poems were used for group worship it was as an incentive for the group to reflect pious attitudes. In secular lyric the same personal mood exists.

Lyric, as its name indicates, began as a musical medium. Aristotle calls lyric 'the music of the flute and lyre', and observes that 'in the music of the flute and of the lyre, "harmony" and rhythm alone are employed; also in other arts, such as that of the shepherd's pipe, which are ... similar to these' (31-32). There is little doubt that Hebrew psalms were also originally set to music. Various psalms have titles that include 'to the chief musician' (e.g. 80, 81, 83, 84, *et al.*), and Ps. 149.3 indicates that music was a large part of praise in worship. While the manner in which these Greek and Hebrew poems were put to music is no longer entirely clear to us, that in no way negates the lyrical, rhythmic nature of the songs.

As opposed to following a story line that includes characters, places, and events, lyrical poems extend no farther than their immediate topic. Cleanth Brooks observes:

> Poetry, however, does characteristically *focus on the feelings and attitudes* in such a context, and not on the actions or ideas as such; this distinction . . . is crucial. As we shall later try to illustrate, poetry is concerned with the massiveness, the *multidimensional quality*, of experience (6).

For example, Psalm 8 states its subject—the excellency of God—in verse one, lists the evidence for the stated subject in vv. 2-8 and closes with a repetition of the subject. No fuller explanation is offered, no opinions are sought other than those of the reflective poet, and no involved plot has developed. While epic narrative and drama are sequential and consequential, thus needing a series of scenes to be coherent, lyric poems exist as self-contained units of 'feelings and attitudes'.

Because lyric poetry utilizes rhyme, parallelism, alliteration, assonance, metaphor, and other devices not normally associated with other genres, or at least not in such a large degree, it is an ornamental genre. Patterns like the acrostics of Lamentations and Psalm 119 are unique to poetry, as is the dirge-like rhythm of Lamentations. Ornamental is meant in the positive sense here, since it is through such poetic devices that lyric achieves its beauty.

Drama is an ancient art form that can be traced *at least* as far back in Greek civilization as 600 BCE, and probably originated earlier in Greece as well as other countries. In Greece, drama developed out of the Dionysian religious cult. Worshipers felt that the adoration for the message of their god could best be demonstrated through dances and choral presentations. As Margarete Bieber writes, 'The Dionysiac religion was from the beginning inclined to disguise individual personality in favor of a transformation into a higher being' (2). Unlike other cults, the worshipers of Dionysius formed creative *myths* about their god, as opposed to merely repeating *rituals* or *liturgies* on a yearly basis (Bieber:1). From these myths grew the stories that were performed at the cultic festivals by the choruses.

As the chorus developed as mythic storyteller, certain innovations began to appear. A leader of the chorus was designated, and often served as the chief singer or speaker for the chorus. This leader also portrayed a god or victim as he spoke or sang. Probably the most important innovation of the early sixth century BCE was the introduction by Thespis of an actor, or character who existed apart from the chorus as an independent figure (Bieber:ix). At first the actor had little to say and the chorus continued to dominate the performance, but as time passed the actor and his struggles became more important. Another innovation was the introduction of drama into the state festivals of Athens in 534 (Bieber:ix). Drama thus became part of national celebrations, and was eventually presented during the Olympic games (Rose:147). Contests were started to recognize the best dramatists.

Soon after drama became part of the Athens festival, the dramatist who best illuminates Zephaniah was born. How or why Aeschylus (524–456) became a dramatist is unknown. What is known is that he emerged as the best dramatist in Greece when he won first prize at the Athens festival in 484, an honor he was to receive 13 times (Rose:147-48). Aeschylus is said to have written 90 plays, of which only seven survive (Rose:148).

The important aspects of Aeschylus' art must be noted at this point. First, Aeschylus introduces the second actor into drama. H.D.F. Kitto says the second actor revolutionized drama because 'he enabled plot to move, to move longitudinally in action, as well as vertically in tension' (1950:34). Kitto further observes:

> The second actor was not intended to be a foil or complement to the first; simply to supply him with the facts to which he was somehow to accommodate himself. There is no interplay between the two (1950:55).

The two actors did not speak extensively *to each other*, but still provided information the other needed.

Second, Aeschylus writes on particularly religious themes such as justice, the wrath of the gods, and the suffering of the human race. While exhibiting the foundational characteristics of drama, much diversity exists in religious drama. It can utilize naturalism or not, vivid characters or not, even gods or not. Kitto concludes, 'That is to say, religious drama is a distinct kind, with principles of its own, different from those of tragedy of character' (1960:233). Thus, religious drama sets its own patterns.

Lastly, Aeschylus gradually de-emphasized the role of the chorus as the importance of the actors increased. Concerning this trend, Bieber says the chorus' 'dwindling importance' continued as a third actor (and subsequent actors) was added (20). It was only because of the success of the second actor, however, that the chorus became less important.

Structurally, Aeschylus' drama has at least three main elements. The dramatist, like the epic writer before him, expects his audience to know the background of his story. That is, the story line is so familiar to his hearers that, for instance, they would know before seeing *Agamemnon* that the major conflict between Agamemnon and his wife Clytemnestra is the fact that Agamemnon sacrificed their daughter to the gods some time previously to win a battle. So Aeschylus assumes a history of understanding of his plot. Another element is that every play has a conflict, or *agon*. Each play has a struggle between two or more parties (e.g. Aegisthus and Clytemnestra vs. Agamemnon in *Agamemnon*). Every one of Aeschylus' plays also has a *denouement*, or climax. Someone avenges or is the victim of revenge, such as when Agamemnon is killed, or a new system of justice is instituted. The drama is therefore brought to an end through the staging of *the* dramatic moment.

From this brief historical survey the complexity of drama is evident. This complexity mirrors life. In fact, Aristotle deems it the most significant of the genres because its imitation of life is so complete (54-55). Drama can assume various modes of expression, such as comedy, tragedy, or farce, but still share common elements. Certainly no two dramas are identical. A comparision of Beckett's *Waiting for Godot* and Shakespeare's *Hamlet* proves that point. Even in all its complexity, however, drama is basically characterized by a unity of plot and character.

Arguments whether plot or character is more important in drama have continued for centuries. The debate cannot be settled satisfactorily. Without strong characters even the best plot collapses and without a good plot characters have no way to develop. Therefore the implications of plot and character will be discussed, but no statements about value will be offered.

Plot encompasses action, place, and time, which are known as the 'three unities', plus all the means of presenting these elements. Unity of action indicates that drama focuses on a specific action rather than a series of events as in epic. As Aristotle says, drama takes 'the form of action, not of narrative' (36). Theodore Hatlen defines action as the movements of the actors, the speeches of the actors, the psychological implications of the plot, and the structure of the plot (22-24). Thus, just because a single action is presented does not make drama simplistic. Usually the play opens with a scene of *exposition* that gives background information about the play's story and characters. The plot's outline becomes visible after the exposition scene. Next, some *complication* arises that creates interest in the plot. Then the extreme *crisis* point of the drama takes place, where the full implications of the play's complications are evident. Finally, the crisis is followed by a solution, called the *denouement*. Action is heightened by points of discovery and foreshadowing that add depth to the story. Thus, action is unified and explained by a continual story line from start to finish.

Unity of place is also vital to drama. Because of the limitations placed on staging a drama, a play is normally restricted to one place, although at times two or three places may be utilized. In epic any place in the world can be a scene, but the visual restrictions of drama make this freedom impossible. Drama gives the impression that the world revolves around the play's place of action.

Closely akin to unity of place is unity of time. A play usually takes place in a short period of time, often within twenty-four hours. Drama not only acts as if the world revolves around its scene, but also that time virtually stands still. If the playwright wants to portray the past he must do it through dialogue. Only in this way can a large amount of action be compacted in a brief period of time. In short, 'the incidents of the plot are *time-bound*, that is, must occur in a given chronological order' (Olson, 1972:35). It is easy, then, to see the differences between narrative, where action, time, and place can be extended indefinitely, and the compact nature of drama.

Another aspect of drama unlike narrative is characterization. Since the playwright cannot offer direct commentary as a narrative writer does, one can only learn about his characters by what they do, by what they say, by other characters' actions towards them, and by what other characters say about them. The dramatist must *show* the audience characters without directly *telling* their faults and virtues. Dialogue is important in characterization, since it allows the individuals to interact with one another by speaking, acting, answering, and reacting.

Many types of characters exist in drama. Symbolic characters are supernatural creatures such as God and angels, or characters that portray non-beings like death, sin, etc. These characters serve as types of the human race. They are truly representative of humanity in their actions. Stereotypical characters 'are built around a single quality or trait' (Berlin:23). They are always the same, never deviating from their inherent stupidity, wisdom, evil, or righteousness. Natural characters are the best developed, because they are free to grow in knowledge and experience and have their personalities altered by their experiences.

It is easy to see that the character must fit the plot and *vice versa* or the author's intention is thwarted. Indeed some characters exist as functionaries of the plot (Berlin:23). Elder Olson explains the importance of this point when he writes:

> The roles of characters will obviously differ in the different kinds of plot. It is quite conceivable, for example, that a consecutive plot should make different demands on character from those made by a descriptive plot, and the pattern plot or the didactic plot may make yet others. And the dramatic form makes a difference both in the functions and the kinds of characters: tragedy requires a different sort of protagonist from comedy, and farce from melodrama. There are always, in addition, the exigencies of the particular work itself (1972:82-83).

Sub-genre

Beneath the umbrella of the three major genres stand sub-genres that grow out of their larger counterparts. Sub-genres arise by taking aspects of drama, narrative, and lyric and developing them in a unique way, and are therefore branches of the major genres. Another way to look at sub-genres is to note particular types of epic, lyric, or drama. By using this method the critic discovers tragedy under drama and the personal lament under lyric. In other words, these are types of literature within a definite kind, or genre, of literary expression.

So many possibilities for sub-genres exist that some limits must be set. Alastair Fowler notes:

> There naturally arises the question of how far subdivision should be taken. For we need not regard the absence of literary terms for the sub-genres as setting a limit. We need not confine ourselves to recognizing only those forms that our predecessors happened to name. However, subdivision beyond a certain stage becomes unwieldy, if only because it leads to as many subgenres as poems (113).

Sub-genres need to have, like genres, elements that distinguish them.

Fowler suggests that sub-genres be divided much like genres (112). That is, sub-genres exhibit the characteristics of their genres, plus some variation of their genres (such as length, scope, or emphasis), and also have enough examples to justify designating a sub-genre. The length of this study does not allow for an exhaustive listing and explanation of sub-genres, but what follows will reflect these criteria.

Epic forms are the hardest to classify into sub-genres. As was stated above, C.S. Lewis divides epic into primary and secondary epic, but these divisions are more according to historical development than sub-genre. Milton's diffuse and brief categories are also hard to categorize, but they have more promise. Milton cites Job as a brief epic (126). This distinction by size shows Milton believes epic elements can be scaled down to a smaller model. Milton himself wrote small epics, at least much smaller than *Paradise Lost*, entitled *Paradise Regained* and *Samson Agonistes*. In each there are fewer characters, a simpler plot, and brief subjects.

Another way of identifying sub-genres of epic is by subject. *The Odyssey* is a travel epic, *The Iliad* a battle epic, and *The Aeneid* a combination of the two. Milton and Spenser wrote epics that deal with universal theological themes. Other examples could be cited, but this methodology suffers from a lack of true epics with which to work, as does all epic criticism.

Lyric lends itself much more readily to sub-genre analysis. Again, forms like the ode and sonnet could be examined, but the Bible offers excellent illustrations of lyric sub-genres, and such illustrations are more relevant to this book. Some helpful literary work on lyric has been done by form critics. These scholars seek to classify the psalms according to their subject, which is related to the discovery of sub-genres. Since most psalms are lyric, and thus reflective in nature, it is important to know the focus of the poets' reflection. Sigmund Mowinckel's *The Psalms in Israel's Worship* describes various psalm forms, three of which are mentioned below. Not *all* the categories presented by form critics are useful to the literary critic, since the designation of some poems as, for example, 'enthronement psalms' leaves the realm of the received text and seeks some pre-textual history. Still, there are places where literary and form criticism intersect.

Hymns of praise to Yahweh are a vital part of Psalms. Such poems normally begin with a call to praise, then include reasons for praise, and end with a final shout of praise. Obvious examples of the hymn are found in Psalms 146-150. Many reasons are given for praising God in the separate poems, including the personality of God, some historical action of Yahweh, or the answering of a personal prayer.

Psalms of personal lament are dotted throughout the psalter as cries for help (Ps. 10), admissions of guilt (Ps. 51), and prayers for vengeance (Ps. 137). The poet usually starts the psalm with a specific problem, elaborates the dilemma, and closes with an assurance that God will help. Each initial cry is from agony of spirit, and the petitions can be either elaborate (Ps. 51) or relatively simple (Ps. 137). Every poem seems to be written with a quiet confidence that God is ready and able to answer the poet's request. God is approached because He alone can solve the dilemma.

Sometimes the reflective poet approaches Yahweh as an intercessor for the nation. These poems take the form of a lament, so they have been entitled national laments. Speaking for the people, the psalmist cries to Yahweh for help (Pss. 12.1; 60.1; 74.1), describes the problems the people encounter (Ps. 74.3-10), and asks for assistance, usually in the form of vindication or vengeance (Mowinckel:193-202). These poems show that the concern of the psalmists extends well beyond their personal needs to include problems of national scope.

Drama has a number of sub-genres. In fact, many of its sub-genres have been considered genres themselves. Tragedy, comedy, satire, closet drama, one-act plays, etc. have existed for so long and have had so many proponents that it is somewhat difficult to call these sub-genres. Still, they exhibit the basic characteristics of all drama in varying degrees, and are therefore types of drama. The large number of examples of these types of drama does, however, help explain their natures.

Tragedy is the father of other dramatic forms. While tragedy is preceded by cultic drama, it is the form that popularized drama and defined its boundaries. Tragedy's most prominent trait is the portrayal of its main character—the tragic hero. Northrop Frye explains:

> The tragic hero is typically on top of the wheel of fortune, halfway between human society on the ground and something greater in the sky. Prometheus, Adam, and Christ hang between heaven and earth, between a world of paradisal freedom and a world of bondage (1967:207).

Tragic heroes are usually superior to the other characters in a story morally, physically, or emotionally. Yet they are not equal to divine beings. Thus, they are balanced between heaven and earth. While they lack the weakness of normal people they also lack the strength of gods. Because he is human, the hero usually fails through some tragic flaw. Achilles' flaw is anger, Hector's is pride, and Faustus' a desire to know what only God can know. In tragedy, the gods try to keep the hero from ascending to their thrones and human beings attempt to drag the hero down to their level. There are, of course, many variations of these patterns.

Other characters in tragedy serve to illuminate the hero's story. Some serve to reveal the strengths or flaws of the heroes. Others exist to move the plot, such as stock characters, messengers, etc. Normally one character serves as foil, or opposite to the hero. This character is usually the hero's enemy, and has a different personality, goal, and function in the plot.

Frye shows that the action in tragedy consists of the righting of balance in nature (1967:209). The hero disturbs the proper balance between deity and man, nature and miracle, and law and obedience. Prometheus steals fire from the gods, thus lessening their mystique but greatly helping mankind. His punishment emphasizes the gods' rule over the earth. Agamemnon sacrifices his daughter to win a battle, which is surely a breach of nature. His death somehow atones for her slaughter. The marriage of Oedipus to his mother opposes all propriety, so his blinding somehow allows law to prevail. Frye concludes:

> The righting of the balance is what the Greeks called *nemesis*: again, the agent or instrument of *nemesis* may be human vengeance, ghostly vengeance, divine vengeance, divine justice, accident, fate or the logic of events, but the essential thing is that *nemesis* happens, and happens impersonally, unaffected . . . by the moral quality of human motivation involved (1967:209).

The result of tragedy, then, is that order is restored. Tragedy is 'an epiphany of law, of that which is and must be' (Frye, 1967:209). Rigid structures are put back in place at the end of tragedy regardless of whether the restoration seems just or not. In fact, a feeling of injustice aids one's sorrow over the hero's fate and adds to the tragedy's effect. On the other hand, when justice is served one's sense of indignation is justified.[3]

It is impossible to equate biblical and Greek tragedy. Greek tragedy is arbitrary in its conclusions. That is, real justice may or may not be served. The gods are both impersonal and ineffectual in Greek tragedy. Their decisions are colored by jealousy, pettiness, and spite at times. Like the characters, the gods are also bound by the unchangeable chain of fate. Characters in Greek tragedy are more like biblical heroes. Both face the problem of being superior to average people, and both suffer the consequences of their choices. Yahweh greatly differs from Greek gods. He is in total control of the universe. He is neither bound by fate nor capricious in His actions. Still, there are tragic elements in the Bible, as is seen in Samson, Job, and David. These elements contribute to the mood of many books, as is discussed below.

Comedy is the foil of tragedy in many ways. Instead of building the play around one heroic character, comedy utilizes a number of figures to present its plot. As opposed to the tragic hero, the comic hero often has a pliable, neutral personality so he can change as the story takes shape (Frye, 1967:167). This does not mean the hero has no goals or convictions, just that he is open to change. He is not bound by fate as his tragic counterpart is. Other characters are more important in comedy because they seek to aid or hinder the hero's desire. For instance, in a romantic comedy the hero may be helped in his wish to marry a certain girl by a clever friend, but thwarted by an ill-mannered, overbearing father of the girl. Thus, other characters determine the success or failure of the hero.

Action in comedy also differs from tragedy. As Frye notes, 'The obstacles to the hero's desire . . . form the action of the comedy, and the overcoming of them the comic resolution' (1967:164). Beyond the gaining of the hero's wish, comedic action seeks to bring about the conversion of those who oppose the hero, and include them in the happiness of the hero and his friends (Frye, 1967:164). Instead of the separation inherent in tragedy, then, inclusion is the goal of comedy. Everyone is won over to the goal of the protagonist. Such inclusion takes place in the works of Aristophanes, Shakespeare, and Shaw, and indeed in all comedy.

Since the characterization and action of comedy varies from tragedy, its result is also different. The result of comedy is to create a world in which conflict is resolved and unity can exist. Character is united to character, society with society, and man with God. This cessation of hostility creates an atmosphere of euphoria and paves the way for utopia. Comedy is therefore much more open-ended than tragedy, where fate and law are served without fail. Normally the audience believes the ending is just and that things are as they should be. Little indignation is felt over the result of the action, so the audience experiences a relief from anxiety (Esslin:73).

There is no *exact* parallel to Greek comedy in the Old Testament. As with tragedy, however, there are many comic elements in scripture, with the chief of these elements being comic action. Resolution, restoration, and reconciliation are as prominent in the Bible as in secular comedy. The prophetic literature particularly seeks to present the separation of Yahweh and Israel and how the two are reunited. In Zephaniah, as in Isaiah, Ezekiel, Amos, etc., Israel's striving against Yahweh exhibits comic futility, as does the rebellion of the nations. Their conversion also leaves hope for the future. Recognition of these common features aids the interpretation of prophetic literature.

Closet drama is a unique sub-genre. It is composed in dramatic style, but is written without the play ever meant to be staged. The author is thereby able to concentrate on poetry and content without worrying about how the play will affect an audience. Many closet dramas exist, with Milton's *Samson Agonistes*, Shelley's *The Cenci*, and Browning's *Pippa Passes* serving as the most famous examples. These plays are usually styled after Greek drama, but often result 'in an eclectic and original adaptation both of the common elements of Greek tragedy and of various special features characteristic of the several dramatists' (Bush:415). For instance, Milton adapts Greek tragedy to fit the story of Samson. Still, closet dramas follow the Greek tradition by limiting action to a single event, by preserving the unities of time and space, and by using choruses and messengers (Hanford:282). Character and action are also similar to Greek drama.

The importance of closet drama for biblical studies is that its existence proves a literary piece need not be staged to be drama. Many objections to speaking of biblical drama revolve around the historical concern of how, where, or if such drama was staged. Closet drama is drama that exists as art without being presented. It thinks, moves, and means as any other play. Its presence leaves open the possibility of exploring literature that has dramatic characteristics, plot, character, dialogue, etc., as drama.

Modes
Fowler's final category for genre study is 'modes', which basically means the way genres and sub-genres are presented (175ff.). A study of modes clears up some lingering questions about genre. The reader may find poetry embedded in narrative or dramatic elements in a lyric section and wonder if generic distinctions are tenable. Or, the reader may wonder what atmosphere pervades a literary work. Many of these difficulties are solved by an understanding of how authors use modes. Modes are located by noticing the mood of a passage or by uncovering the limited use of a genre within another genre.

Various moods are created by writers, including comic, tragic, and ironic. Since many of the aspects of comedy and tragedy appear in an earlier section they will be presented more briefly here. The comic world is one in which a happy ending is assured for fulfilled characters in an ideal society. Conversion of evil characters often occurs in comedy. Struggles arise on the way to bliss, but they are always overcome. A comic mood insures an open-ended conclusion for a story.

Tragic mood arises out of the author's desire to instill in the readers a feeling of loss, shock, remorse, or outrage. The tragic hero exhibits qualities superior to other people, yet never receives all the victories due a person of great stature. In the Old Testament, Moses' inability to enter Canaan is a tragic moment, as is Adam's sin in the Garden. Samson is tragic in that he is an unusually blessed character whose appetites hasten his downfall. In each of these cases the reader is saddened by the misfortune of a character one wants to see succeed. Thus, loss, shock, and remorse appear in the story line. In the case of the prophets, especially Jeremiah, sadness is replaced by outrage. Prophets tell the truth, but are punished for their message of salvation.

Irony is the presentation of incongruity between what is expected and what happens, between what should be and what is, and between what is said and what is meant. As Edwin Good says, 'Irony, then, begins in conflict, a conflict marked by the perception of the distance between pretense and reality' (14). Job says wisdom will die with his friends, but means they are fools. Jonah expects God to destroy Nineveh, but is disappointed. The heathen sailors in Jonah are more righteous than God's prophet, and Haman is hanged on gallows meant for Mordecai in Esther. Irony drives home points about evil or righteousness. It is not so much an attempt at humour as a means of surprising, correcting, or encouraging the reader.

Irony is notoriously hard to identify because of its kinship with sarcasm and satire. Irony is almost always very subtle, however, so it should not be equated with these more obvious moods. Wayne C. Booth offers five keys to identifying irony. Irony exists when there are:

1. Straightforward warnings in the author's own voice;
2. Known errors proclaimed;
3. Conflicts of facts within the work;
4. Clashes of style; or
5. Conflict of belief (1974:57-76).

Again, incongruity is the key to spotting irony. The first two keys are obvious incongruities, while the last three keys are much more hidden. When any of these five items exists the author is telling the reader more is happening than appears on the surface.

Each of these moods molds a tone for lyric, drama, and epic. They are not genres or sub-genres but make them what they are. Other moods, such as satiric, could be discussed, but these three are the most common in scripture. To summarize: if the writer desires to encourage a comic mood may appear; if instruction is needed irony can be used; if repentance is the aim tragedy may be employed. Of course other uses of these modes occur, but these examples help explain why one mode is used in a situation and not another.

Short portions of one genre may appear within another genre to produce a specific effect. In 2 Samuel 22-23 lyric appears to sum up David's gratitude for God's care. Psalm 78, although poetic, recounts the history of Israel as a narrative section might to emphasize Yahweh's mercy. Dramatic scenes appear frequently in prose narrative and lyric. Joseph's being thrown in the pit and his brothers' bowing before him are dramatic scenes that show the character of the men without directly telling the reader. Boaz's bargaining for Ruth is another dramatic passage. Song of Songs is a drama written in lyric poetry to preserve the passion of romantic love. Again, these mixings of genres do not obliterate the main genre, rather they emphasize a major feature of that genre.

Summary

This chapter establishes a classicist method of discovering Zephaniah's genre by surveying historical trends in genre studies, exploring the characteristics of biblical prose and poetry, and explaining the literary traits of the three classical genres. These general ideas about genre are complemented by specific studies of sub-genre and mode. A careful analysis of Zephaniah can now be made. When a close reading of the book is completed the results can be compared to each genre, sub-genre, and mode and a comprehensive understanding of its literary nature gained. Thus, like chapter 1, this part of the book provides a framework for analyzing Zephaniah.

A most important caution arising from the historical survey is that genres are not rigid, monolithic structures. Each literary artist uses a generic medium to reveal creativity and individual style. Still, genres *do* exist and inform literary study, and it is legitimate to search for Zephaniah's place in classical categories.

Chapter 3

A CLOSE READING OF ZEPHANIAH

Chapters 1 and 2 provide a methodological foundation for exploring Zephaniah. The first chapter states the need for both close reading and genre analysis in a thorough literary study, and the second chapter explains genre study. This chapter attempts a close reading of Zephaniah to reveal its literary artistry and provide information about its genre. As was stated in the first chapter, 'close reading' means the careful evaluation of the major aspects of a literary work. While some facets of Zephaniah are not mentioned, the points covered reflect the main elements of Zephaniah.

The Structure of Zephaniah

Edgar V. Roberts defines structure as 'the organization of a literary work as influenced by its plot . . . or main idea. . . . The word is also sometimes defined as the pattern of emotions in the literary work' (119). Every literary analysis needs to deal with structure, since themes, images, ideas, and actions must be revealed through a literary framework. A work's structure should be one with the other elements of the art form. That is, it should be appropriately chosen in consideration of genre, plot, characterization, and imagery. A well-chosen structure allows these components to blend in a logical fashion. As Roberts declares, 'In a good work of literature, the parts are not introduced accidentally. One part demands another, sometimes by logical requirement' (120). Finally, an effective structure is cohesive and unobtrusive. Kitto says that in the best literary work 'the component parts are grouped in one unalterable way; the composition has what the Greeks called *rhythm*, and it never occurs to us that we should mentally recompose it' (1966:16). Since structure is so interrelated with other parts of a literary piece there is some overlap between a discussion of structure and the explanation of other literary aspects in this chapter. An effort is made, however, to keep such overlap to a minimum.

Biblical scholars have dealt quite inadequately with the structure of Zephaniah. Most merely posit some sort of three-part scheme, as if the book has a superstructure but no substructure. S.R. Driver reduced Zephaniah to three convenient parts: Destruction (1.1-18), Repentance (2.1-3.7), and Restoration (3.8-20) (1891:341-42). Childs divides the book into threats against Judah (1.2-2.3), threats against the nations (2.4-3.8), and promises to each (3.9-20) (458). Other writers outline the prophecy according to its individual threats of judgment (Ralph Smith:124), or its threats *and* its redactional layers (J.M.P. Smith:172-74, 182ff.). Even commentators who deal more carefully with this aspect of the work fail to notice the subtle structural shifts the writer employs. In short, these commentators may deal with themes, or major movements in the text, but they hardly explain *structure*.

One must discern the intent of a structure before making statements about it. Usually, as noted above, a work's structure reflects its plot. Stated briefly, Zephaniah's plot revolves around the writer's concept of 'the day of Yahweh', and the prophecy's framework is chosen to reveal this idea. Clyde Francisco recognizes that Zephaniah offers many notions about 'the day of Yahweh', including that the day is imminent (1.14), a time of terror (1.15), a judgment for sin (1.17), and a disruption of nature (1.15). It will fall on all creatures and all nations (1.2-3; 2.4-15), and will be survived by a remnant that will enjoy the blessings of Yahweh (2.3; 3.9ff.). Bernard De Souza lists more of these characteristics, and sums up the 'day' as an expression of God's wrath (12-17). Thus, it is the intent of the structure of Zephaniah to gradually introduce these plot elements. This process allows the plot's conflict and resolution to unfold in an orderly fashion that lets tension build throughout the book.

Dialogue in Zephaniah

Zephaniah's framework is built on dialogue between Yahweh and the prophet that forms seven sets of speeches in the text. These speeches are evident because of the writer's shifting between first- and third-person narration. Several commentators note the presence of two speakers in Zephaniah. Gerhard von Rad realizes that the book displays 'a continuous change in style between objective descriptions of events and words spoken by God in the first person' (1965:122). Moulton states that, throughout the prophecy, God denounces Judah, but that 'this denunciation is at intervals interrupted by snatches of verse, not words of God, but lyric comments upon the divine word at emphatic points' (124). Kapelrud correctly divides the speeches by the use of first- and third-person designation for Yahweh. He observes:

> Whatever the origin of the two styles of speech was, it is hard to find any other differences between them in Zephaniah than the purely grammatical one that one speaks in the first person singular, the other in the third person (48).

Kapelrud argues that the presence of two speakers does not mean there are two redactional layers of the text, one in first and one in third person (48). While this belief may be true, Kapelrud rejects the idea that there is *any* significance in the existence of the two speakers. He concludes that 'the division between divine and prophetic speech is irrelevant in Zephaniah. It does not add anything to a better understanding of the message of the prophet' (49). Kapelrud errs at this point, however, since these speeches are the key to the book's structure. The speeches' presence, then, is unchallenged, but their significance has gone unnoticed.

Each set of speeches consists of a speech by Yahweh and a speech by the prophet, except that Yahweh, fittingly, has the last word.[1] Of course the characters speak for a reason, since the speeches reveal plot, movement, characterization, and genre. As Holman claims about dialogue:

> (1) It advances the action in a definite way and is not used as mere ornamentation. (2) It is consistent with the character of the speakers, their social positions and special interests. . . (3) it gives the impression of naturalness. . . (4) It presents the interplay of ideas and personalities among the people conversing; it sets forth a conversational give and take—not simply a series of remarks of alternating speakers. (5) It varies in diction, rhythm, phrasing, sentence length, etc., according to the various speakers participating. (6) It serves, at the hands of some writers, to give relief from, and lightness of effect to, passages which are essentially serious or expository in nature (528).

Holman's survey of dialogue underscores its importance for plot, characterization, and themes. Holman also establishes that speeches have many lengths and purposes. In Zephaniah the characters do not speak directly to one another, but, as in early Greek drama, the characters supplement and complement each others' words (Kitto, 1950:55). All seven sets of speeches are examined to show how they form the book's structure.

Set one. Yahweh's first speech (1.2-6) establishes the tone for the first five series of speeches. Total judgment is announced. All of creation, including men, birds, and fish, is to share in the destruction. The reason given for the destruction of the earth is that the people have ceased to follow the Lord (1.6) and have begun, or continued, to serve other deities alongside Yahweh (1.4-5). God is obviously quite angry at the present state of affairs, and His words come with great suddenness and vehemence.

Recognizing Yahweh's extreme anger, the prophet's first speech (1.7) cautions the audience to be silent before the Lord. No defense for their actions is acceptable, and no protest is allowed. He also announces the prophecy's governing theme, the day of Yahweh. Thus the structure reveals plot in the initial round of comments. The prophet further mentions that a sacrifice is being prepared and that Yahweh has selected His guest. Such imagery would be familiar to early readers of Zephaniah.

Set two. His anger still raging, Yahweh interrupts the prophet and begins His second speech (1.8-13). Here He condemns everyone in Israel from 'the princes and king's sons' (1.8) to men who believe God will do nothing good or bad about the nation's actions (1.12). General apathy about God exists in the land, which the writer conveys with sight and sound imagery. Yahweh is shown here as all-knowing, since He sees all the corruption in the land.

Continuing his initial theme, the prophet now elaborates on the day of the Lord (1.14-16). Three basic components of the day are revealed: its imminent nature (1.14); its terrifying aspects (1.15); and its disruptive character (1.15). Once again the sober prophet solemnly warns the audience of its fate. At this point the oblique reference to 'sweeping away' is already an event with definite contours.

Set three. God's speech (1.17) is shorter and less vitriolic than the previous two, but it still declares that the people's sin will cause them to become 'dust and ... filth'. In this round of orations His short speech sets the stage for the prophet's first long speech.

The prophet's third series of remarks (1.18–2.7) is vital to the scheme of the play, for he inserts two more aspects of the plot, which are the possibility of escaping judgment and the condemnation of other kingdoms. To this point no hope for averting the wrath of God has been offered; rather, the entire world is to be destroyed. In the midst of this hopelessness the prophet mentions that the 'humble of the land' may, perhaps, be saved (2.3). This group of people becomes the remnant from whom God forges a new, righteous nation (cf. 3.12-13). The author uses this piece of foreshadowing to offer insight into the end of the play.

Nearly as important as the possibility of forgiveness is the knowledge that Israel's enemies will also be judged on the day of the Lord. The reader therefore learns that all nations are responsible to God. Israel is given some encouragement, for the land of the enemies is promised to the remnant (2.7). Once more the writer anticipates the last two series of speeches by speaking of the remnant's exaltation. Expectation is thereby heightened. In the midst of conflict, resolution is in sight.

Set four. Since it has been the prophet who has provided the new schematic elements, Yahweh is now in the unusual position of filling out *the prophet's* message (2.8-10). In this way the two characters work as interchangeable revealers, and the word of the two is shown as one united word. Because of the pride of Ammon and Moab (2.10) they too will receive severe punishment (2.9). Also, Yahweh himself now mentions that the remnant will plunder their enemies. More light, then, is shed on the darkness of absolute, devastating judgment. Very briefly (2.11), the prophet mentions that the nations are judged because of their idols. These gods will have to pay homage to Yahweh. This verse is to be read with 1.4-6, because both denounce foreign gods. The sin of Israel and her neighbors is linked as one and the same. This idea is renewed when Israel and Assyria are compared (cf. 2.13–3.5).

Structurally, the fourth series of comments serves as a pause in the action. No startling new factors are introduced, no further characterizations made, or clever insights offered. This set is really a lull before the storm of activity in the concluding orations. Once more anticipation is raised, this time by a lack of statements instead of an abundance of them.

Set five. Not wanting to forget even one enemy, the Lord includes Ethiopia in His judgment (2.12). Such a statement precludes the possibility of God being unaware of the nations' sins.

In another long speech (2.13-3.5), the second actor compares
Israel with Assyria, traditionally one of her most bitter enemies.
Ninevah is to be just as devastated as Moab and Ammon (cf. 2.9 and
3.14). The once-great city becomes a place despised by all. Just at the
point at which the reader is enjoying the destruction of Assyria,
however, the author reverses his line of thought to show how Israel is
similarly wicked. Every level of society in Israel is unresponsive to
God. Officials and judges are corrupt, prophets are 'wanton', and
priests 'profane' (3.3-5).

Clearly the plot's conflict is now fully presented. It finds its
summary in this fifth speech of the prophet. Israel and the nations
stand together in direct opposition to God. For His part, the Lord is
sending judgment on all offenders. As has been seen, however, this
conflict can be resolved through repentance.

Set six. Yahweh himself begins the resolution (3.6-13). It has been
His purpose to judge and destroy (3.6-8), but now the author unveils
the final element of his plot, the mercy of God. The day of Yahweh
will conclude with the grace of Yahweh. His grace is extended first to
all the nations. They will receive the opportunity to 'call upon the
name of the Lord and serve Him with one accord' (3.9). In return,
Yahweh will purify their speech (3.9).

More importantly, for Zephaniah's audience, the Lord will take
away the shame of Israel and forgive the nation's sin. A purging
process must take place, whereby the old, proud people are removed
in favor of a humble, holy remnant, but this process benefits the
nation (3.13). Another integral part of the plot is now in place.
Yahweh's remnant has moved into the realm of reality.

Likewise, the prophet encourages the audience to rejoice in the
presence of God ('in your midst') and his plans for restoration (3.14-
17). Once more the two characters are partners in revelation. Both
have proclaimed judgment, and now both join in the announcement
of the remnant's rise and the nation's resulting restoration. God will
act as warrior for Israel and rejoices over them (3.17). The prophet's
final speech completes his character. At the start of the book he was a
warning figure, while at the end he is an exhorter of the people.
Thus, he is the complete prophet, combining judgment and salvation
in his message.

The pleasant turn of events does not totally surprise the reader, for
the author hints at Yahweh's redeeming work in 2.7 and 2.9. All
tension built over the threatened judgment is relieved as the

foreshadowing changes to fulfilled promise. By using this method of interrelating promise and completion the book's structure is tightly bound by allusion and concrete image.

Set seven. Only Yahweh speaks in 3.18-3.20. At this point He summarizes His acts of grace by saying He will deal with Israel's oppressors, save her cripples, and bring her scattered people home. The prophecy's plot is now also complete. It seems a strange ending, for the book's beginning suggested an unhappy conclusion. The writer shows his artistic skill by changing the expected into something surprising and different. Zephaniah is not allowed to degenerate into an oracle of total doom, which saves the work from being a dreadful, hopeless mass of condemnation.[2]

Throughout Zephaniah the book's structure effectively unfolds the intended plot. Each set of speeches has an artistic purpose, whether it is to present a problem, heighten suspense or tension, or conclude the work with a satisfactory resolution. Both speakers are important, for each actor's part is versatile enough to initiate plot elements or buttress the comments of the other. These structural achievements point to an author with a definite plan for presenting his story, and one who can carry out his plan with subtlety and ingenuity.

The Plot of Zephaniah

Much of Zephaniah's plot is presented in outline form in the preceding section. A great deal more, however, can be said about the story line of the book. This section will also analyze the prophecy by working through the seven sets of speeches, but will focus on the *intricacies* of Zephaniah's conflict and resolution. Plot involves both what happens in a story and why it happens. As E.M. Forster writes:

> Let us define a plot. We have defined a story as a narrative of events arranged in their time-sequence. A plot is also a narrative of events, the emphasis falling on causality. 'The king died and then the queen died' is a story. 'The king died, and the queen died of grief' is a plot. The time-sequence is preserved, but the sense of causality overshadows it (86).

The key to good plot analysis, then, is to go beyond the events of the story line to the reasons for those events.

Every plot has two major aspects: conflict (*agon*) and resolution (*denouement*). A story's conflict is its great problem. Several problems could exist, such as personality conflicts, national disputes, cosmic arguments, and personal internal struggles. Attitudes, actions, or words can cause this conflict. Resolution is the way the conflict is settled. It can progressively grow out of the text, and thus be an expected solution, or it may come as an unexpected twist in the story. How the author uses these two components largely decides the shape and effectiveness of his plot.

Two kinds of action heighten plot. First, there is rising action that brings the story to a peak and then sustains the peak long enough for the resolution to occur. Rising action is characterized by foreshadowing future events in a way that heightens interest in the end of the story. This interest is sustained whether it is fear, dread, or joyous expectation that stimulates the reader. Second, there is falling action, which creates pauses in the plot and concludes a story after the conflict and resolution are complete. Falling action allows the reader to relax from the tension of the rising action, and also provides explanatory material about the resolution. Both types of action are necessary for a well-rounded plot.

In Zephaniah conflict is apparent early in the book. Zephaniah opens with the specter of judgment. God emphatically states that the time has come to reverse the creation process and totally devastate the earth. All that will be left after this 'sweeping' is rubble (1.3). In Gen. 1.20-26, birds, fish, animals, and men are created, but now they are to be destroyed through the judgment of Yahweh. While the whole creation is threatened, Judah is singled out for punishment in the first speech. The cause of their condemnation is their idolatry and infidelity (1.4-6). Thus, the conflict is between the judge of all creation, Yahweh, and the covenant nation. Israel has bound herself to God alone (Exod. 20.1-6; Deut. 6.4-9), but now turns to other gods. In particular, despite the teaching of prophets like Elijah and Hosea, the nation still maintains some measure of Baal worship. According to John M.P. Smith:

> Baalism died hard in Israel. . . Nor is it necessarily a diluted form of Baalism with which we have here to do, a Baalism cloaking itself under the guise of Yahwism, a syncretism wherein the outer shell of Yahwism was filled with the inner spirit of Baalism. It was rather an unadulterated Baalism which Zephaniah denounced. The out and out idolatry named in the following verse (v. 5) points to this direction (187).

Judah's idolatry includes worshipping the gods of the stars, mixing allegiance to Yahweh and Molech, and failing to seek a word from the Lord. With such apostasy evident in the nation, Yahweh's anger is understandable and his judgment justifiable. Israel's reversal of covenant agreement causes a reversal of creation.

Yahweh's first speech begins the pattern of the story's rising action. The plot moves from the general announcement of judgment to specific reasons why judgment takes place. From these specific reasons more specific judgments are mentioned. The prophet's declaration that 'the day of the Lord is near' is very general in scope, and is clarified throughout the prophecy, but would still strike fear in the reader's heart because of earlier prophecies about the 'day'. Isaiah's utterances on the day of Yahweh are similar to Zephaniah's (Isa. 2.11ff.), since both speak of judgment brought on by idolatry. The prophet's brief speech therefore causes anxiety merely by giving God's wrath a name and a context.

More and more recipients of judgment are named as the second speeches are made. God mentions in His first speech the doom of idolatrous priests and star-gazers (1.4–5), and now every segment of society is included as well. The royal family is judged because of their emphasis on foreign life-styles (1.8). Worshippers are condemned for improper temple practices that bring 'violence and deceit' into God's house (1.9). Likewise, wailing rises from every element of society: the rich, merchants, and money traders (1.10-11). Singled out for special attention are people who believe Yahweh is a powerless, apathetic deity (1.12-13). Yahweh's dispute with the nation is more specific now. He is dissatisfied with every possible kind of citizen. His complaint entails more than idolatry, with apathy, violence, and dishonesty prime reasons for judgment. *Who* God will judge is now spelled out, but *how* He will judge remains unclarified.

Just as the Lord explains who is to be judged in His second speech, the prophet defines 'the day of Yahweh' more fully in his. Chief characteristics of this day include its closeness (1.14), bitterness (1.14), ability to cause distress, despair, and gloom (1.15), murderous intent (1.15), and comprehensive nature (1.16). Not only will the whole nation be judged, it shall absorb great suffering in the process. Tension is heightened at this point through the nation's total lack of hope. Yahweh's brief third speech punctuates the prophet's comments. Judgment is so complete that it takes on grotesque proportions (1.17).

Zephaniah's third speech begins in the same vein as his previous one, but is interrupted by some falling action. Rather than continue his elaboration of the day of Yahweh, he pauses to exhort the nation to repent. Even this bit of mercy has a biting tone, however, since the author implies Judah has no closer relationship to Yahweh than other countries. As John D.W. Watts observes:

> The people of God are usually called a 'people' and the word 'nation' is used mainly for the heathen so that it became a synonym for 'heathen'. But here, Jerusalem is deliberately classed with the foreign nations, as it will be again in 3.1-7. It has become so foreign in its ways that it seemed to belong more to them than to God (164).

Because of their apostasy, Judah's privileged status is revoked. The only remotely kind word in this pause is to the 'humble of the land' (2.3). If this group seeks righteousness and humility it may be spared.

This pause in the prophet's third speech serves many functions. In the midst of the gloom of the first three speeches it inserts a shred of hope that at least some portion of Judah may be spared. This bit of hope introduces the reader to the 'humble of the land', who become the remnant of 2.7, 3.13, and 3.20. The remnant seeks meekness, righteousness, and the Lord, and receives the blessings of Yahweh (2.3; 3.11ff.). Kapelrud writes:

> In Zephaniah 3.11ff. the dominating view is clearly that the poor and humble people were the truly righteous, while the proud and haughty were considered as enemies of Yahweh. It is out of the question to measure the degree of humility; it is a quality which can hardly be quantified. In the world of Zephaniah it seems to refer mainly to people without influence, without wealth and notable rank in society. In his eyes they were the people who attained righteousness (2.3), the only ones who had a chance to stay alive through the Day of the Wrath of Yahweh (33).

Introducing the hope the remnant provides foreshadows the positive ending of the prophecy. At this point the reader cannot see the victory of 3.14-20, but there is some break in the gloomy picture. One reason it is unacceptable to divide 3.14-20 from the main body of Zephaniah is that several passages foreshadow that ending. Finally, 2.1-2 attempts to shock and insult Judahites into joining the remnant. Such as it is, this biting invitation is the book's first offer of redemption. Some resolution to the conflict is in sight. Rising action can now resume, leading to the ultimate crisis point, but it continues with the whole plot now in focus.

The prophet's third speech concludes with a new part of the plot, the judgment of foreign nations. Yahweh is in control of all peoples. Zephaniah singles out Philistia, a traditional enemy, as the first recipient of condemnation, and others are added later. Each of the enemies named represents a geographical location. Ralph Smith asserts:

> Judgment against Judah's neighbors is the major motif of this section. Philistia on the west, Moab and Ammon on the east, Ethiopia or Egypt on the south, and Assyria to the north will all experience the judgment of Yahweh. Even though Judah's near neighbors were infringing on her borders, she (Judah) would eventually dispossess them (135-36).

Regardless of a nation's location or prowess God is their judge.

Yahweh adds the familiar names of Ammon and Moab to the list of doomed nations in His fourth speech.[3] Two clear reasons are given for the judgment of Ammon and Moab. The first is that they reproached God's people (2.8). Because of Judah's troubles these neighboring countries believed that God had forsaken His People. Second, since they despised Judah's supposed weakness, liberties were taken with her borders. Both nations have forgotten that to despise Judah is to despise God Himself. The Lord sums up such actions as pride (2.10). Like Sodom and Gomorrah, Moab and Ammon will be totally destroyed. This speech contributes to the plot's conflict. God's quarrel is with all sinful nations instead of just with His covenant people. It also continues the story's rising action by adding more and more candidates for destruction.

Once more Zephaniah provides a slight pause in the plot. In his brief fourth speech he explains that the foreign nations will have their gods destroyed and will learn to serve the Lord (2.11). When their false gods are removed the heathen can properly worship. This verse prefigures 3.9, where the nations call on the Lord with 'one consent'. John M.P. Smith claims this stress on universality 'far transcends the reach of faith in Zephaniah's time and indelibly stamps the verse as later' (229). Such historical distinctions are unnecessary when the part foreshadowing plays in Zephaniah is understood. Like 2.1-3, this verse prepares the reader for the prophecy's ending.

God's fifth speech adds the southern country in the list of foreign countries. His short speech basically matches the size of the prophet's preceding oration. This announcement of Ethiopia's doom leads into the prophet's long speech on Assyria, and thus pushes the plot to its final presentation of conflict.

To complete the plot's conflict the prophet chronicles the fate of Assyria, and compares God's people to this pagan nation. The overthrow of once-powerful Assyria reveals that Yahweh is in control of even prominent lands. Assyria's downfall is particularly pleasing to Judah, since Assyria sacked Samaria and besieged Jerusalem. God again avenged His people. As with Moab and Ammon, the great sin of Assyria is pride, for she has said that there is no nation like herself. The result of Assyria's pride is total desolation. All her cities will be emptied, her riches depleted, and her people scattered (2.13-15).

Before the reader enjoys Assyria's condemnation too much, however, Jerusalem is compared to Nineveh. Nahum and Jonah reflect the shame of such a comparison. Nineveh is called 'the rejoicing city' in 2.15, and Jerusalem 'the oppressing city' in 3.1, thus linking the two by the common designation 'city'. Assyria's pride is balanced by Judah's disobedience, lack of faith, lack of devotion, injustice, and perversion of the Law (3.2-4). In many ways God's people surpass Assyria in doing evil. Every segment of Judah's leadership is condemned: princes, prophets, and priests. No doubt this speech intends to shame the nation into repentance, as 2.1-3 does. It also reveals that no matter how angry He may be with pagan nations Yahweh's chief complaint is with Judah. Other countries pridefully reject the Lord, and will pay for their sin, but the fact that Judah is Yahweh's covenant people makes their sin even more unacceptable.

After the fifth set of speeches the plot's conflict is fully presented. Both Judah and her neighbors stand against God, and will therefore be utterly destroyed on the day of Yahweh. A battle line is drawn between the prideful nations and the creator of those nations. One by one the offending nations are named and God's case against them stated. There is absolutely no hope for them, or creation, to stand. Hints at hope surface, though, in 2.3, 2.7, 2.9, and 2.11, indicating that there may be some way to avoid judgment. The tension in the plot is extreme at this point, so some resolution is needed.

Ironically, the plot's resolution is identical to its conflict, the day of the Lord. While the day of judgment punishes the wicked (3.6-8), it also paves the way for the remnant and their future blessings (3.9-13). Yahweh explains in this crucial sixth speech that He punishes nations to get them to repent (3.6-7). This plan fails because the people continue to sin (3.7). One final, cataclysmic day of wrath is therefore planned to dissolve all sin against the Lord. Such a judgment partially resolves the plot's conflict, but still leaves open the fate of the 'humble of the earth' mentioned in 2.3. Since all sinful people are removed in 3.8 the faithful remnant can now serve Yahweh with no hindrance. The remnant shall return from far lands (3.10), find forgiveness (3.11), remain faithful to God (3.12), be righteous (3.13), and dwell in peace (3.13). All these blessings are possible because the wicked are destroyed, therefore allowing the remnant to serve Yahweh in peace.

Zephaniah rejoices in Yahweh's resolution of the great conflict in his sixth, and final, speech (3.14-17). The story now exhibits falling action because Yahweh is vindicated and the remnant is established. Since the conflict is now ended, the prophet encourages Jerusalem to rejoice in what has happened. Through the unexpected salvation provided by the day of Yahweh her sin is forgiven, her enemies are defeated, and her future is secured (3.15). Again, the reasons for their deliverance are God's satisfaction with the remnant and Yahweh's own power to save (3.17). Zephaniah is not stunned by this turn of events because of his earlier comments in 2.3 and 2.7. The remnant, however, requires constant assuring that their fortunes have changed, as is evidenced by the promises of 3.10-13, 15-20. This falling action functions as a summary of the prophecy. It explains to a bewildered remnant what has happened and discloses Yahweh's pleasure with them. It also lets the reader know that all tension between the Lord and the nations is removed.

In the final speech of the book God echoes the statements of 3.14-17. He will restore the nation to its place as the greatest of people. All wrongs are now righted. Throughout the resolution of the plot both Yahweh and the prophet emphasize the fact that the solution to the conflict is *God's work*. Certainly the remnant has a part to play, but it is the *Lord's day* that solves the prophecy's ultimate problem. Yahweh is thereby the maker and controller of the story line.

While some tragic (cf. 2.13-15) and ironic (cf. 1.12-13) elements exist in Zephaniah the book conveys a comic plot. God's purpose for Judah is implicitly stated in the story. He wants Judah to be a nation that serves Him. That purpose is thwarted by the sin and idolatry of Judah and her neighbors. Through the work of Yahweh, the severity of His day, and the salvation of the remnant, however, the Lord overcomes the obstacles to His purpose. Judah is restored, and even the heathen nations, those outside God's covenant, are invited to join the new society created by the day of the Lord. Justice and mercy prevail in this very inclusive plot instead of a sense of rigid law. In fact, the expectation of God's legalistic intractability is exposed by the plot's resolution. Joy prevails rather than a sense of fate.

Characterization in Zephaniah

Characterization is a vital, but often neglected, aspect of literature. In lyric and epic, the writer has the luxury of telling the reader directly about the nature of a character, revealing character through the words of another character, or letting a character show his own nature by his words and deeds. Since the first option is not normally open to a dramatist, characterization in plays depends on the writer's ability to make a character vivid through speeches and actions alone. A *character* is created by an author to be realistic and to fit his plot. Edgar V. Roberts suggests:

> We may define *character* in literature as the author's creation, through the medium of words, of a personality who takes on actions, thoughts, expressions, and attitudes unique and appropriate to that personality and consistent with it. Character might be thought of as a reasonable facsimile of a human being, with all the qualities and vagaries of a human being (45).

On the other hand, characterization is the manner in which a character is presented. Characterization includes the many facets of the character. Roberts correctly observes that characterization 'is the sum total of typical qualities and propensities in any given individual that are controlled by that individual's drives, aims, ideals, morals, and conscience' (44). In other words, a character is a person in a story and the characterization of that person reveals his true nature.

Two methods of exploring characterization are employed in this study. One is to examine character traits by what a character says about himself, by what other characters say about him, and by what he does. This obvious way of looking at characters yields a basic picture of the person. A second, more subtle, method is to note the development of a character as the plot progresses. In this way more imperceptible components of character are uncovered. The consistency of the author's portrayal of his characters can also be checked. There are two characters in Zephaniah, as has already been seen. Yahweh and the prophet (Zephaniah) both give speeches that unfold the book's plot. Each have a distinct personality and a measure of character development. They mention other people (cf. 1.12), but they are the only participants in Zephaniah's action.

Yahweh is, of course, the central character in the drama. He dominates the action with a power fitting to the Hebrew concept of their God. The Lord is from the outset a universal deity. That is, He does not merely reign over Israel, but over all the earth. It is the whole earth He proposes to 'sweep away' (1.2), and He promises to punish foreign nations as well as Israel. Yahweh allows no rivals (1.4-6), punishing those who worship pagan gods (1.5).

Supreme knowledge is also part of Yahweh's character. He knows the thoughts of people (1.12-13) and the attitudes of nations (2.8-10). God responds to what He knows about the human race. Even as Yahweh is cognizant of the sins of the nations, so He is aware of the transgressions of Israel.

Overwhelmingly, in Zephaniah, Yahweh is more a character of action than words. This action initially means judgment of sin. When the Lord recognizes the sin of Israel and her neighbors, His reaction is to 'sweep away', 'bring distress', and 'be terrible against them'. Those who say, 'The Lord will do nothing, either good or bad' (1.12) will be greatly surprised. His power enables Him to act so decisively. The prophet's speeches agree with these statements Yahweh makes about Himself. Zephaniah's first speech warns the nation to respect the 'Sovereign Lord' (1.7) who prepares a sacrifice of evil people. His second speech declares that God's action is a result of His wrath, and will result in gloom and destruction (1.14-16).The prophet's third oration includes foreign enemies in Yahweh's judgment (2.4-7). After a short fourth comment about the destruction of all idols (2.11), Zephaniah's fifth speech shows the comprehensive nature of God's devastating work. Finally, the prophet declares the Lord's saving actions (3.14-17). In every one of his speeches the prophet emphasizes what God *does* and *will do*.

Despite Yahweh's punishing impulse, mercy is a major component of the Lord's character. George Adam Smith disagrees by writing:

> Note the absence of mention of the Divine mercy. Zephaniah has no gospel of that kind. The conditions of escape are sternly ethical—meekness, the doing of justice and righteousness. So austere is our prophet (58).

Smith's view overstates the role of the remnant's repentance in
God's show of mercy. The remnant is encouraged to seek meekness
and righteousness in 2.3, but no mention is made of any overwhelming
turn to the Lord. It is God's decision to cleanse them through the day
of Yahweh that releases them. Yahweh's decision to spare any is a
great mercy in Zephaniah, since the apostasy of Judah is well
documented. From this mercifully spared remnant a new nation will
emerge, for whom Yahweh will defeat all enemies, remove all
disasters, and restore all fortunes (3.11-20). There is even mercy for
Israel's enemies, since all these are allowed to call on the Lord's
name (3.9). Hope therefore springs out of judgment. The prophet's
final speech, particularly 3.17, reflects the generous nature of God.
Thus, the speeches of the prophet work together with Yahweh's
actions to clearly state God's merciful nature.

Throughout Zephaniah, Yahweh is presented as the character by
whom and for whom the drama exists. The artist depicts Yahweh as
he must: as a powerful deity capable of controlling the play's plot,
imagery, and tone. No character should overshadow the Lord, and
the author prevents this from happening. While the prophetic
character is not a stock or flat character, the writer makes sure
Yahweh is the maker and resolver of the plot's conflict.

Within the story line of Zephaniah there is a definite development
of Yahweh's character. The Lord is a much fuller character at the
end of the prophecy than at the beginning. In chapter one Yahweh
bursts into the story as an angry deity who desires to smash the
works of His own hands. The world He has made will be destroyed
(1.2-3), and the nation He has created will likewise be devastated
(1.4-6). Judah's sin justifies this wrath, but in no way lessens it.
Yahweh's anger escalates through His third speech (1.17). Nine times
in those three speeches He says 'I will' do something (cf. 1.2, 3, 4, 8,
9, 12, and 17), with each phrase growing more adamant in its
condemnation of the people. The angry Yahweh first promises three
times to 'sweep away' various parts of creation (1.2-3). Growing
more specific, He says He will 'stretch out' His hand against Judah
and 'cut off' their false worship (1.4). More vehemently, the Lord
claims He will 'punish' specific offenders such as princes and temple
worshippers (1.8-9). In 1.12 He pledges to search out any who expect
to escape judgment. Finally, Yahweh will 'bring distress' to the
nation, making them like blind men and pouring their lives out like
'dust and dung' (1.17). From a general 'sweeping' the specific threat

to make the people dust and dung emerges. Certainly no clearer picture of God on a rampage is possible.

After the third speech, however, Yahweh's anger is somewhat abated. His anger is switched from Judah to the foreign countries. The prophet declares judgment against Judah's enemies, and Yahweh supports these statements with His fourth and fifth speeches. One sign that His anger at Judah has eased is that He condemns Moab and Ammon for mistreating Judah (2.8-10), thus shifting some of His wrath from Judah. God is still, supremely, a judge, but He is now a judge inclined to see some chance of releasing the defendant. In fact, Yahweh categorically states that His remnant will plunder Moab and Ammon and possess their land (2.9). This promise is hardly the threat of a deity wholeheartedly opposed to Judah. Thus, the totally wrathful picture of God of 1.9-17 is tempered by the portrayal in 1.18–2.12 of Yahweh as still angry, but now offering a bit of hope.

The Lord's character develops even more in 2.13–3.20. In His last two speeches, God's anger is completely spent and is replaced by an attitude of mercy. The nations and Judah are judged in 3.8, but 3.9 begins Yahweh's restoration, or re-creation, of the earth. To contrast the God of 3.9ff. with the God of 1.1-17, the author presents a new series of 'I will' sayings. Each of these sayings is a positive statement of God's kindness to Judah and, surprisingly, the nations. He promises to 'purify the lips of the people' so they can serve Him (3.9). Such a statement is astonishing in the light of His comments in 2.8-10 and the prophet's declarations in 2.4-7 and 2.13–3.5. Further, Yahweh will remove the proud from Jerusalem so the 'meek and humble' remnant can rule the city (3.11-12). A final burst of promises comes in 3.18-20, where the Lord declares He will remove burdensome feasts and oppressors, 'rescue the lame' and give them honor, and gather the scattered people to restore their fortunes. God's restoration of the nation in chapter three is as complete as His destruction of the world in chapter one. He is now a judge who pardons.

Yahweh's radical switch from merciless judge to restoring creator is dramatic but not totally unexpected. Because of His endorsement of the remnant (2.8-10) the reader is prepared for further moves towards mercy. The author skillfully presents Yahweh as a character who develops as the plot progresses. His character is one with the conflict and resolution of the story, as well as its tension and rising action. The Lord is still the judge of the earth when Zephaniah ends, but the emphasis is now on a merciful judge. He is not an unstable character, however, since it is through this developing mercy that His purpose of judgment is best completed.

Less complicated, but still vitally important, is the author's characterization of the prophet. Like Aeschylus' early second actors, he is somewhat of a 'flat' character in that his personal thoughts and emotions are hidden from the audience. There is never any indication of whether Yahweh's plans are pleasing to him or not. What this characterization intends, though, is to present the second character as the ideal prophet. He speaks about Yahweh rather than himself. He fills out the message of the Lord instead of injecting his own feelings into the story. At all times his major task is to interpret God's message to Judah. He is concerned for the nation (e.g. 1.7), even in the face of its sin. The prophet obviously trusts Yahweh's will, for he resonates with Yahweh's statements and stands with God against the sin of the world.

By serving as the faithful prophet, the second character fulfills a vital artistic function. Without him the plot has no human touch. With him, though, God's ways are made evident to the human race through Yahweh's own speeches, but also through the prophet's understanding of God's words. The second character thus helps the plot progress by adding a horizontal dimension to the story's vertical images.

The prophet says nothing about himself, nor does Yahweh address his character. Thus there are no direct comments on his personality. Like Yahweh, however, his character is made plain by his speeches. The prophet (Zephaniah) is characterized in three ways: interpreter of God's wrath, proclaimer of world-wide judgment, and herald of Judah's restoration. His character also develops as the plot progresses. Unlike Yahweh, he is most developed in the middle speeches rather than at the beginning or end. The author balances his plot by making the prophet prominent where Yahweh is more quiet.

Zephaniah's first words come between Yahweh's first two wrathful speeches. The prophet quickly explains that the people must be hushed before God because 'the day of the Lord is near' (1.7). This explanation of God's anger shows Judah the seriousness of her sin. After God's second caustic speech the prophet describes Yahweh's day in fuller detail. The day is imminent (1.14), bitter (1.15), and a day of wrath (1.15). He lists several facets of the judgment, including distress, anguish, trouble, ruin, darkness, gloom, and battle (1.15-16). No doubt is left about the severity of the coming punishment. In both speeches Zephaniah's role is to explicate Yahweh's wrath to the audience.

In his next three speeches the prophet reaches his full stature as a character. He no longer merely interprets the Lord's speeches, instead he offers the knowledge that foreign countries will share in Judah's judgment. It is Zephaniah who first mentions the hope for the faithful remnant (2.2, 7). It is the prophet who denounces the old enemies Philistia and Assyria, claiming both will be desolate (2.4-7; 2.13-3.5). Zephaniah still stresses, however, that it is *God's* judgment he is announcing (cf. 2.2-3; 2.11, 13; 3.5). Yahweh remains the story's principal figure. Still, the prophet is now an original proclaimer of judgment instead of just an interpreter.

Finally, the prophet serves as herald of Yahweh's merciful restoration of Judah and the nations (3.14-17). Like a choral leader, the prophet encourages Judah to sing of God's redemption (3.15) and love (3.17). Once more he interprets the message of God, but this time as a joyful proclaimer of good news. Zephaniah's final role also radically changes from beginning to end. In 1.7 he counsels the people to be silent because of their sin, but in 3.14 he encourages them to sing about their salvation. The gloom of 1.14-16 changes to the exultation of 3.14-17. Despite the lack of personal comments by Zephaniah, the development of his character is evident. As with Yahweh, his character fits the flow of the plot. His changing character matches the evolving nature of the book's conflict and resolution. Though very little can be said about the prophet's personality traits, his ability to fulfill several functions shows he is obedient, versatile, and totally prophetic.

Themes in Zephaniah

Great themes permeate literature making the artistic piece take on subtlety and complexity. C. Hugh Holman defines a 'theme' as,

> The central or dominating idea in a literary work. In non-conflict prose it may be thought of as the general topic of discussion, the subject of the discourse, the thesis. In poetry, fiction, and drama it is the abstract concept which is made concrete through its representation in person, action, and image in the work (528).

Holman's definition is only adequate for noting the end product of a theme. That is, he says, when totally drawn a theme is a major subject, idea, or concept. This definition leaves out, though, the way themes are constructed in a work. Wilfred Guerin explains that themes are composed of images, symbols, actions, and personalities. These smaller units of thought interact with one another to create a larger thematic unit.

> Thus motifs are not just matters of diversified image; they can be diverse actions or episodes, different personalities, or mixtures of pictures, meditations, and symbols. But always the disparate items blend; they fuse or synthesize. And our realization of the synthesis becomes the joy of discovering what we already have dimly perceived (157).

Since, as Guerin indicates, imagery, actions, and personalities are the major aspects of themes, a study of these elements in Zephaniah reveals how the book's main motifs are composed. Imagery is 'any verbal appeal to any of the senses; a stimulation of the *imagination* through sense experience' (225). Both visual and aural imagery appear in Zephaniah. By 'action' is meant the deeds of characters in a story (e.g. Zeph. 1.12-13). The personalities buttress themes in the plot. For instance, God's judgment is made more believable by His obvious anger.

Quite obviously, the great theme of Yahweh's day of judgment dominates the prophecy. Indeed all other themes come and are inseparable from it. Nearly every commentator on the book emphasizes the primary nature of this theme, and a great amount of literature has appeared on the day of the Lord. Within the confines of this book it is impossible to chart every aspect of the day of Yahweh in the Old Testament, so only Zephaniah's concept of the day is covered, and only the high points of his portrayal can be mentioned. The theme of God's day of judgment has two major facets. Obviously, the first of these facets is destructive judgment. Just as vital, though, is the reconciliation brought by the judgment.

Total judgment is presented through a series of vivid imagery. The first image is 'the sweeping' of the earth (1.2-3). Human beings, birds, fish, and animals will be destroyed in this cleansing of the earth. A visual image of absolute emptiness is projected. John D.W. Watts believes this image parallels 'Noah's flood even in the choice of words (cf. Gen. 6.8)' and that 'Zephaniah's new word from God seems intended to replace the promise of Gen. 8.21' (156). Michael De Roche notes Watts' argument, but finds another Genesis parallel in 1.2-3. He concludes that

> The crux of Zephaniah's oracle, however, is that he reverses the order of these beings from that in the creation account. Thus, Zephaniah is not simply announcing judgment on mankind, nor is he only disqualifying Yahweh's promise of Gen. viii 21. Zephaniah is proclaiming man's loss of dominion over the earth, and more importantly, the *reversal of creation* (106).

While De Roche's argument best matches the book's context, both opinions fit the spirit of Zephaniah's image, since Noah's flood certainly resulted in a reversal of creation. The purpose of the image is to show the totality of Yahweh's angry judgment. One by one, every creature on earth is removed from the scene.

Other visual images that follow the judgment theme are the darkness of the day and the distress that accompanies the darkness (1.15, 17). Because of God's wrath distress, anguish, trouble and ruin will grip the human race (1.15). This promise of the prophet is reinforced by Yahweh's speech in 1.17. Distress is justified because 'their blood will be poured out like dust and their entrails like filth' (1.17). Darkness, gloom, clouds, and blackness cause the people to become as 'blind men'. This gloom is caused by God's wrath in heaven and by war on earth (1.14, 16). Personal *and* national darkness and distress are indicated. Thus, Yahweh's 'sweeping' of creation casts the world into utter blackness. Once more prehistoric times come to mind, for before the first day of creation 'darkness was over the face of the deep' (Gen. 1.2).

Much more extensive is the visual image of desolation. Perhaps more than any image this one conveys the idea of God's ability to judge. Note the following descriptions of various nations.

1. Judah (1.13): houses demolished, uninhabited houses, untended vineyards;
2. Philistia (2.4-7): abandoned, in ruins, emptied, none left, a place for shepherds and sheep pens;
3. Moab and Ammon (2.9): like Sodom, like Gomorrah, a place of weeds and salt pits, a wasteland forever;
4. Cush (2.12): slain;
5. Assyria (2.13-15): utterly desolate, dry as the desert, a pasture for flocks and herds, a haunt for roosting owls, a

place where calls echo, rubble is abundant, and beams are
exposed, a ruin, a lair for wild beasts, a place of scoffing;
6. Nations in general (3.6): demolished, deserted, devoid of
traffic, destroyed, totally empty.

The totality of judgment is driven home with shattering force by
these pictures. Cities that stand against Yahweh are emptied. Men
who stand against Him are slain. Nations too proud to serve Yahweh
are brought to their knees. 'Sweeping' and 'darkness' lead to the
desolation of the nations.

Various *actions* add to the judgment theme. Yahweh's main action
is that of controlling history. He can sweep away the inhabitants of
earth in the future because He created them at the beginning of time.
God also manipulates the movements of nations. Warriors fight and
battles rage because they are instruments of judgment (1.14-16).
Chapter two clearly declares Yahweh's authority over countries, and
indicates that their downfall is caused by their attitude towards the
Lord and His people (cf. 2.10-11). The Lord also rules the future, for
the day of judgment ushers in a new era of peace for the faithful
remnant (3.13-20). An understanding of Yahweh's control of history
furthers the judgment motif by removing any notion that the
devastation chronicled by the book's imagery is a historical
coincidence. Everything mentioned is part of God's judgment of
Judah and the world.

Controlling history is a very general action, but more specific
actions of Yahweh appear in the text. *Individual* countries and
persons are mentioned as objects of wrath. Various kinds of nations
are singled out for obliteration. As was stated earlier, there is a
definite geographical scheme in the naming of Philistia, Moab,
Ammon, Cush, and Assyria. Beyond this connotation is the fact that
each is a traditional enemy of Judah. Philistia represents an old and
deadly enemy of both Judah and Yahwism. This nation has fought
every Israeli leader from Joshua onward. Moab and Ammon are also
ancient foes, but unlike Philistia these peoples are near kin of Judah
through Lot (Gen. 19.36-38). Rather than a close family ally,
however, these nations revel in Judah's defeats (cf. Ps. 137.7 and
Zeph. 2.8-10). Cush holds some historical significance, but Assyria
represents a major opponent. Assyria captured Samaria and nearly
overthrew Judah during Hezekiah's reign. Unlike the other countries
named it had enjoyed worldwide influence. The point of censoring
these countries is to prove that any type of enemy of God and Judah

will be destroyed by the day of Yahweh. General 'sweeping' includes the devastation of particular places.

Particular people are doomed as well: religious officials, royalty, and the common citizen. Yahweh's action comes first against priests who mix the worship of Yahweh and pagan gods. The Lord totally rejects such syncretistic practices, saying such priests and worshippers 'turn back from following the Lord and neither seek the Lord or inquire of him' (1.6). To place God on the same level with other gods is to reject Him altogether. Royalty will be punished too. 'Princes', 'king's sons', and 'those clad in foreign clothes' are rejected for much the same reason as the worshippers. The reference in 1.8 to foreign attire indicates Yahweh's displeasure with an acceptance of foreign customs in Judah's court. Just as foreign as their clothing is their worship. As Frank Eakin observes:

> Following closely as this does upon the condemnation of astral worship . . . we recognize that the acceptance of foreign clothing conveyed more broadly a life-style which would have inevitably included foreign worship (279).

Again, syncretism leads to judgment. The Lord judges common people who no longer believe in His power, who say God will do nothing about Judah's sin (1.12). These people are described as so 'complacent' they resemble 'wine left on its dregs'. S.R. Driver says this simile means:

> sunk into a state of moral stagnation and spiritual indifference. The figure is taken from wine, which, after the process of fermentation was complete, was left upon its sediment or 'lees' (Is. XXV 16) only long enough to fix its colour and body. If not then drawn off, it grew thick and syrupy—sweeter indeed than the strained wine, and to the taste of some more pleasant, but feeble and ready to decay (1906:118).

While not overtly evil, the laziness and unbelief of these people bring the wrath of God on them as surely as it comes on the idolaters. Yahweh will show how wrong it is to mistake His patience for a lack of power.

God's actions, then, affect every person and nation on earth. Priests, royalty, common people, Judah, and pagan nations alike will bear the brunt of His indignation. The Lord does not merely pass mental judgment, as if making a moral assessment, instead He acts out His outrage. Because He is the creator of the world and possessor of great power He is able to carry out His threats. Always people are punished for their sin, so their destruction seems just.

A final strand of the judgment aspect of the day of the Lord comes through the personalities of Yahweh, the prophet, and the people. As stated in the characterization section of this chapter, anger is a main trait of God in the first half of the book. The cause for His anger is the sin of Judah and the nations. Probably the clearest statement of this indignation is in 3.8, where he decides 'the whole world will be consumed by the fire of my jealous anger'. His wrath is also revealed throughout Zephaniah by the following action images where He says He will:

1. Sweep away (1.2-3)
2. Cut off (1.3 and 3.6)
3. Punish (1.8, 9, 12)
4. Wipe out (1.11)
5. Search and punish (1.12)
6. Plunder (1.13)
7. Bring distress (1.17)
8. Destroy (2.5)
9. Slay (2.12)
10. Remove (3.11)
11. Deal with all ... (3.19)

Yahweh's personal anger leads to the actions He takes. His speeches in the story reflect the author's purpose of showing that the day of Yahweh is an awesome time to be feared by the whole creation. When God is angry the whole creation trembles.

One other kind of personality reflects the judgment theme, and that is the personality of Judah and her neighbors. Both are rather contemptuous of Yahweh. Judah thinks God is powerless (1.12), so she serves other gods (1.4-9). Since the nations view Judah as weak, they further assume Judah's God is weak. Yahweh and Judah are therefore mocked and insulted (2.10). Assyria's power causes that nation to say, 'I am, and there is none besides me' (2.15). Such pride forgets the creator of the universe. Because of their attitude these nations are ripe for judgment. They are also deserving of judgment, which makes the author's theme much easier to portray.

The images, actions, and personalities in Zephaniah make clear the book's theme of the judgment of the day of the Lord. Fearful, devastating judgment is coming because of the sin of the human race.

Even God's people are caught up in this sin and will participate in God's wrath. Page Kelley summarizes the judgment theme very well:

> The fury of that day will be focused on those who have sinned against the Lord. Their destruction will be both horrible and inescapable. It will be so horrible that their blood will be poured out as if it had no more value than dust and their flesh as if it were as cheap as dung. It will be so inescapable that neither silver nor gold will avail to deliver sinners from the wrath of the Lord. All the earth will be consumed and all the inhabitants of the earth will come to an end (95).

This gloomy picture is not the only theme, however, that is inherent in the day of the Lord. Through judgment emerges the grace and mercy of Yahweh. Several images contribute to an opposite portrayal of God's work. An initial image is that of the remnant of Judah lying down like sheep in the wasteland that was once Philistia (2.7). Before this pastoral image Yahweh cares only about Judah's destruction, but now He is their shepherd who creates a resting place for His 'sheep'. Another image is the purifying of the nations' lips (3.9) so they can call on the Lord properly. In a miraculous turn of events the heathen are allowed access to Yahweh. Until this point only 2.11 gives any indication that God cares for Judah's enemies. Now God shows mercy. One more significant passage reveals imagery portraying the new theme of grace. In 3.14-17 the prophet encourages Judah to 'sing', 'shout', 'be glad', and 'rejoice' over God's redeeming work. A party or festival is proclaimed, for God is 'with' the people once more (3.15). Yahweh joins the people's singing in 3.17 and soothes them by His love. A loving parent is pictured in this passage. Certainly Zephaniah shows the day of Yahweh as a time of great destruction, but from the destruction unfolds a theme of forgiveness (cf. 3.8-9).

God's action furthers the mercy theme. His first action is to leave open the possibility that a select remnant can survive the day of the Lord (2.3). If these people are humble and righteous—significantly different than the rest of the nation (cf. 1.4-13)—they may be spared. God's second action is to promise to care for the nation and 'restore their fortunes' (2.7). All creation deserves destruction, but God will protect a remnant. Closely aligned to the 2.7 passage is 2.9, where the remnant is not only spared, but allowed to plunder enemy countries. To fully prepare the remnant to rule, a third action is required.

Yahweh will remove the proud from the midst of the remnant (3.11), and then leave only the meek and humble (3.12). A fourth, and most decisive action, is that the Lord will 'rescue', 'gather', 'bring home', and 'honor' Judah. This final act completes the restoration of God's people. The possibility of a redeemed remnant has become a completed picture of a new and powerful people. Once judgment is fully meted out in 3.8 it becomes an avenue for the mercy of God.

Certain actions of the remnant mirror the goodness of Yahweh. The remnant *does* exhibit some humility and righteousness or God would not champion their cause. They are morally superior to the wicked of the earth because of their humility. S.R. Driver says 'humility' refers to

> an attitude towards God, and denotes one who *bows* or humbles himself under the hand of God. The word is often used in the prophets and Psalms . . . of the pious and faithful worshippers of Yahweh, as opposed to the 'wicked' the 'evil-doers', the 'proud', etc. (1906:122).

Such humility leads to an active trust in the Lord (3.12). Their integrity is impressive, for they 'do no wrong', 'speak no lies', and are devoid of deceit (3.13). They praise God for His mercy, and thus show their dependence on Him (3.14-17). From the point at which potential mercy is offered to the remnant, they become progressively more acceptable to God. Their actions follow the deeds of Yahweh in a significant way. Because of His mercy the remnant becomes what Israel should always have been. God's goodness bears fruit.

As is obvious from His actions, the personality of the Lord reflects the mercy that emerges from the day of Yahweh. New concepts establish His kindness:

1. He is with Judah (3.15)
2. He removes fear (3.15)
3. He delights in the nation (3.17)
4. He quiets the people (3.17)
5. He rejoices over Judah (3.17)
6. He rescues and gathers the nation (3.19)
7. He gives Judah honor and praise (3.20)
8. He restores their fortunes (3.20)

It is the will of God to restore, comfort, and gather the nation after judgment falls. This conciliatory impulse is quite different from the wrathful Yahweh of the earlier section of Zephaniah. Wrath is not forgotten, rather it is eliminated through the completion of judgment (3.8-9). Mercy enters through the remnant as well, thus saving a portion of the human race.

Part of Yahweh's mercy is displayed in His inclusion of the pagan nations in the worship of the Lord. One of the by-products of the coming devastation is the turning of the heathen to Yahweh. When He destroys their cities and gods they learn to serve Him (2.11). When His wrath is totally spent He will purify the foreign people so they can serve Him (3.9). While the nations are not promised as much as the remnant, the fact that they can come to Yahweh at all is an incredible offer. Idolaters and enemies of God and His people are made as acceptable as Israel. There is no greater evidence of the Lord's kindness in the entire book, and it is this kindness that best defines His personality.

The prophet's personality also illuminates God's character. Even before Yahweh declares His intention to spare the remnant and create a new world for them the prophet confidently proclaims God's redemption of the remnant (cf. 2.3, 7). It is the prophet who first mentions the inclusion of the nations (2.11). Zephaniah has an attitude of complete confidence in the mercy of Yahweh. Just as the prophet warns Judah about coming judgment (1.7), so he foresees the grace of the Lord. After the prophetic word God does what the prophet predicts. Thus, while Yahweh announces judgment, it is the prophet who is the forerunner of kindness.

Such a brief discussion of the themes in Zephaniah in no way covers the great motifs of the book, but the discussion does demonstrate how themes fit together and complement structure, plot, and characterization. The conflict and resolution of the plot, judgment and comic reconciliation, are brought to life by the themes of condemnation and mercy. The theme of God's judgment mirrors the rising conflict of the plot, and the theme of mercy reflects the unusual ending of the story. Neither plot nor theme can exist without the other.

Characters are also illuminated by themes. The gradual development of God's character reveals the change from total wrath to total inclusion. The prophet's confidence in the Lord is fitting for God's prophet, and God's actions justify Zephaniah's faith. Yahweh's power is emphasized in the book's major themes, as is the prophet's role of provider of new information. In short, all parts of the prophecy make the artistic work a coherent whole.

Point of View in Zephaniah

Few areas of literary criticism are as complex as point of view. Various methodologies have been posited for examining this subject, many of which vary a great deal. Point of view is the discipline of finding who tells a story, how it is told, how accurately it is told, and with what amount of knowledge and understanding it unfolds. All these elements reveal the position from which an event is seen and narrated. As can be seen from the definition mentioned above, two subjects comprise the main concerns of point of view: who tells the story and how it is told. The former concern is normally covered under discussions about narrators and the latter under treatments of narration.

R. Alan Culpepper shows that three terms are crucial in the telling of a story: real author, implied author, and narrator (15-16). The real author is the person who actually pens the contents of a literary work. There is no need to discuss the real author of Zephaniah in this dissertation. This author's identity is not a trivial matter in a historical study of the prophecy, but this dissertation analyzes the literature the real author produced, not the real author.

An implied author is the person the author chooses to embody thoughts, feelings, and values in a story. Wayne Booth says, 'The "implied author" chooses, consciously or unconsciously, what we read; we infer him as an ideal, literary, created version of the real man; he is the sum of his own choices' (1963:74-75). Booth further adds:

> Even the novel in which no narrator is dramatized creates an implicit picture of an author who stands behind the scenes, whether as stage manager, as puppeteer, or as an indifferent God, silently paring his fingernails. This implied author is always distinct from the 'real man'—whatever we may take him to be— who creates a superior version of himself, a 'second self', as he creates his work (1963:151).

The implied author is the writer pictured by the reader, or the writer as implied by what is emphasized in a story. Real author and implied author may or may not have similar beliefs depending on the needs of the story.

A narrator is the person who actually tells the story. Unlike the implied author, who is behind the text, the narrator stands within the text as a story teller and interpreter of events. Three types of narrators are prominent in literature. A first-person narrator 'refers to himself as "I", or, like Flaubert, tells us that "we" were in the classroom when Charles Bovary entered' (Booth, 1963:152). This type of narrator speaks as an eye-witness. Another kind of narrator is the third-person narrator, who describes individuals in the story as he, she, it, they or them. The third-person narrator is often called the omniscient narrator, since this type speaks not as an eye-witness, but as an all-knowing chronicler of events (Holman:336). Finally, many works narrate by using a dramatic approach. No intrusive voice appears in the text. Instead, the speeches and actions of characters set up and explain events in the story. Edgar V. Roberts thinks:

> A writer using the *dramatic* point of view confines his work mainly to quotations and descriptions of actions. He avoids telling you that certain characters thought this or felt that, but instead allows the characters themselves to voice their thoughts and feelings... The key to the dramatic point of view is that the writer presents the reader with action and speech, but does not overtly guide the reader toward any conclusion (57).

Different literary works vary as to how much the implied author says and knows. One first-person narrator may be more intrusive than another. A third-person narrator may have more knowledge than a like narrator in another story. Some works are more effective with dramatic narrative than others. The reliability of narrators differs as well. Because of better knowledge, information, understanding, or motives some narrators are superior to their counterparts. When the type of narrator is discovered his accuracy must also be determined. In other words, how the story is told by the narrator is examined. These are the core concerns of narration. It is not enough to recognize the narrator without understanding his narration, or narrative technique, as well.

Culpepper borrows three facets of narration from Boris Uspensky that help explain how a narrator works (21-34). Psychological point of view 'is determined by whether or not he or she is able to provide inside views of what a character is thinking, feeling, or intending' (21). Spatial point of view is contingent on how many people and places the narrator can view at once (26). Ideological point of view explains the values of a narrator (32). The last aspect is especially vital in a norm-forming book like the Bible. These areas help focus the implied author's function as well as the narrator's.

One final factor affects the implied author, narrator, and narration, and that is the implied audience, or narratee (Berlin:52). If the implied author and the narrator have a purpose in what they say, then it is also true that they aim at a certain kind of audience. The implied audience is that group of people that seems to be set forth by the narration. They are the recipients of the values proclaimed by the implied author or narrator.

One key to understanding and discovering Zephaniah's implied author and implied audience is to chart the 'distance between the essential norms of his implied author and the norms of the postulated reader' (Booth, 1963:157). Many of these norms have been noted in previous sections of this chapter through the discussion of plot, characters, and themes, and are reinforced here. In Zephaniah the implied author attempts to expose the audience to a way of thinking about Yahweh and acting on His commands that is foreign to their present actions.

The implied author in Zephaniah speaks about the present and the future. In this way he is thoroughly prophetic. Many things about the present trouble the implied author. The nation has become syncretistic in its customs (1.8) and in its worship (1.4-13), and is in danger of losing its distinctive identity as God's people. Some segments of the nation trust in wealth more than the Lord (1.13, 18). Foreign nations sin against Yahweh and His people (e.g. 2.8-10) without realizing the consequences of their actions (3.8). Throughout the prophecy the implied author stands against these sins, and is particularly opposed to idolatry and syncretism. The future is seen by the implied author in two ways. One way is the possibility of total destruction brought on by the sin already mentioned. If there is no repentance only judgment can fall (1.2-3). If there is repentance by Judah and her neighbors, however, forgiveness may come (cf. 2.3 and 3.9). This second way of presenting the future offers hope to the implied reader of the book.

Despite his negative comments about Judah, or perhaps because of them, the implied author is very pro-Judah. It is obviously the hope of the implied author that judgment can be averted and the nation preserved. Before this preservation can happen there must arise a humble, repentant remnant (2.3) that learns to do God's will (3.12-13). God must purge the land of all people unwilling to join the remnant (3.11), and God must purify the nations so they can serve Him (2.11 and 3.9). Through these actions Judah can be gathered and have her fortunes restored (3.20). The fact that the book ends with a long passage dedicated to the preservation of Judah hints at the implied author's care for God's people (cf. 3.14-20). This care and concern extends even to Judah's ancient enemies.

By being pro-Judah the implied author is also entirely pro-remnant. From its first mention in 2.3 the implied author encourages the remnant to take its place in the restoration of Judah. The remnant is encouraged by threats (2.3), promises (2.7, 9), praise (3.12-13), and assurances of God's love (3.14-20). Without the remnant there is no hope for Judah, so it is imperative for the implied author that the remnant know and accept its role. To be pro-remnant, then, is to be pro-salvation and pro-restoration.

The implied author is also greatly in favor of Yahweh's plan to purify and re-create the earth through the day of Yahweh. No defense of the people's actions is offered, and even the remnant must meet certain moral requirements. If no remnant could be found, then the implied author is therefore totally aligned with Yahweh's righteousness, wrath, and mercy. God's purpose and tactics are never questioned (cf. Habakkuk), not even when Yahweh includes pagan nations in the plans for the restored world (cf. Jonah). Such unquestioning faith reveals an explicit trust in the Lord.

Quite different from the faith-filled, righteous, disciplined implied author is Zephaniah's implied audience. This audience embodies all the sins the implied author denounces. It is depicted as idolatrous (1.4-6), syncretistic (1.8), materialistic (1.13, 18), proud (2.15), lazy and complacent (1.12), and ripe for judgment. The inhabitants of Jerusalem are 'oppressors, rebellious and defiled' (3.3), 'arrogant', 'treacherous', 'violent', and 'profane' (3.4). There is no praise for the religious leaders (prophets and priests), since they do not teach the truth. This implied audience is not confined to Judah, though, because other nations are condemned and offered hope for the future. Philistia, Moab, Ammon, Cush, and Assyria are all addressed in Zephaniah, which adds an international flavor to the implied audience. These nations sin against God and Judah, but will be punished and cleansed by the day of Yahweh.

Even with all the implied author says against the implied audience there is some hope for it. Buried beneath a great deal of sin is the possibility that some of the implied audience has historical opportunity for change. That is, the implied author indicates that the implied audience is not in a political or economical situation that is so terrible that a healing of the nation is impossible. Political and personal opportunity still exists. The audience is therefore corrupt nationally and individually, but is not beyond the hope of redemption.

Now that the ethical positions of the implied author and the implied audience have been sketched, it is possible to explore how these positions are narrated. Of initial importance is the voice of Zephaniah's narrator. There is no first-person narration that comes from outside the action itself. Yahweh speaks in the first person many times. He refers to Himself with 'I' 29 times,[4] 'my' 8 times,[5] and 'me' 3 times.[6] These references come from an active character, however, rather than a narrator speaking about actions and characters from personal knowledge or experience.[7] The prophetic character never uses a first-person pronoun in his speeches, preferring to speak exclusively of Yahweh's actions.

Some possibility of outside third-person narration exists in the work. The first verse of Zephaniah stands outside the action of the book, and functions as an indicator of the prophecy's historical setting. This verse implies a seventh-century seting for the work. Six other verses reveal a third-person narration (1.2, 3, 10; 2.9; 3.8, 20). In each of these verses the declaration 'says the Lord' punctuates Yahweh's statements.[8] The first three occurrences of the term emphasize the judgment of God against the earth (1.2), the human race (1.3), and Judah (1.10). The fourth usage emphasizes Yahweh's swearing by His own name (2.9). A fifth appearance of the phrase highlights the purging nature of the day of Yahweh (3.8), and the final occurrence of the term ends the book (3.20). All six appearances of 'says the Lord' alert the reader that Yahweh is speaking, but beyond that point is the fact that the major themes of Zephaniah, judgment and mercy, are set apart by this phrase. Only very pivotal speeches of Yahweh are chosen to receive this linguistic emphasis.

Third-person narration is very minimal in Zephaniah, even with the presence of its use in 1.1, 2, 3, 10; 2.9; 3.8, and 20. Beyond the first verse only one highly stylized phrase is used in the third person. Third-person phrases serve a function in the story, but do not dictate the flow of the book in any significant way. Therefore, third-person narration cannot be viewed as Zephaniah's chief mode of narration.

Zephaniah's principal method of narration is dramatic presentation. An implied author has created the characters and their situation, but leaves it up to the characters themselves to present the action of the story. It is Yahweh who announces the day of the Lord and explains its meaning. It is the prophet who fills out God's announcement of judgment by telling of the devastation of Judah's neighbors. It is the prophet who suggests Yahweh may be merciful. It is Yahweh who purges the earth to bring about the world's restoration. It is the Lord who includes the foreign nations in the remnant. Every action in the plot is announced and carried out by a character in the book. No outside narrator explains or completes the action. Certainly Zephaniah does not say 'that certain characters thought this or felt that, but instead allows the characters themselves to voice their thoughts and feelings' (Roberts:57). Of course the characters themselves react to one another's speeches and explain what the other says, but these aspects are part of the dramatic presentation rather than a separate narrative technique.

As was stated earlier, psychological, spatial, and ideological points of view help explain a work's narration. Since Zephaniah exhibits dramatic narration the traits of its characters explain these narrative aspects. From a psychological viewpoint Yahweh is omniscient in Zephaniah. He knows the thoughts of the people of Judah (1.12) and of the nations (2.8) and assesses judgment for them. The prophet also understands the thoughts of at least one nation (2.15), so he shares in Yahweh's knowledge. Yahweh knows the future, because He directs it, and allows the prophet to know His plans (cf. 1.7; 1.18–2.7; 2.13–3.5; 3.14-17). Nothing escapes the attention of the two characters. Both know the remnant, and both give the remnant assurance of its place (3.14-17).

Because of their omniscience it is logical that the characters are also omnipresent. Yahweh observes the actions of Judah (1.4-13), Philistia (2.5), Moab and Ammon (2.8-10), and Cush (2.12). He hears insults (1.12 and 2.8) and sees evil that people do (1.4-5, 12). Likewise, the prophet realizes the shame of Judah (2.1; 3.1-5) and Assyria (2.13–3.5). The prophet also knows what Yahweh will do. He mentions the saving of the remnant (2.3), the mercy that will be afforded the nations (2.11), and the completion of Yahweh's work (3.14-17). Both Yahweh and the prophet seem to anticipate and understand the statements each makes. They can either be in the streets of Jerusalem (1.12, 3.1-5) or present with the remnant (3.14-20). This spatial viewpoint offers a comprehensive idea of why judgment is coming and how it is used for the good of the remnant.

Ideologically the characters are reliable. They build a strong case for the necessity and correctness of judgment through the chronicling of the sins of Judah and her neighbors. If this portrayal were inaccurate the prophet would have presented the remnant as worthy of redemption much earlier than he does. The fact that Yahweh is a character in the story indicates that the implied author assumes the reliability of God's statements, as does the presence in the work of Yahweh's prophet, who knows Yahweh's plans. In fact, Zephaniah is presented in a way that precludes any possibility other than reliable narration.

In summary, Zephaniah's implied author calls for a sinful implied audience to repent and become part of a small remnant that escapes a great day of judgment. The implied author and audience are far apart in their ethical standards, but there remains some opportunity for the audience to change. Dramatic narration is the major mode of telling Zephaniah's story. Yahweh and the prophet reveal every aspect of the plot, and do so in a way that demonstrates their omniscience, omnipresence, and reliability. The implications of this point of view become clearer in Chapter 4.

The Time Sequence in Zephaniah

Within the three major genres two very distinct time sequences are evident. In epic, one scene follows another in a reasonably sequential way so a story can proceed from beginning to end. Great periods of time are presented. Empires can rise and fall within the confines of epic, especially when it sums up the past, but the action always takes place within a relatively short span of time. Lyric presents time as lasting as long as it takes to read the poem. Old Testament passages reflect different time sequences too. Kings and Chronicles present a sequential narrative, but the psalms use a lyric time frame.

Zephaniah's action unfolds in a seemingly eternal or timeless present. The threat of judgment, the offer of mercy, and the achievement of restoration occur in rapid fashion. There is no time element involved even though restoration follows judgment sequentially. Action is telescoped in Zephaniah, which means there are no long narrative explanations like in Samuel, Kings, Chronicles, or any of the other Old Testament histories. The scope of the book extends thematically to the judgment and restoration of all creation, but is presented in a very compact way. Zephaniah's whole message can be heard and grasped within a few minutes' time.

Summary

This chapter is the pivotal part of the thesis. Every major aspect of Zephaniah is analyzed to provide data that will uncover the book's genre. Several important ideas emerge. First, Zephaniah's structure is created by a series of alternating speeches. Second, its plot has a definite conflict and resolution. Third, its plot is shaped by an overwhelming emphasis on the 'day of Yahweh'. Finally, an almost totally dramatic point of view pervades the book. Each of these conclusions provides important clues to the genre of Zephaniah, and will be compared to the three classical genres in Chapter 4.

THE APPLICATION OF GENRE THEORY TO
THE CLOSE READING OF ZEPHANIAH

Chapter 2 offered a way of understanding and using genre theory. Chapter 3 explored the literary aspects of Zephaniah. Now that theory and data have been presented, it is necessary to unite the two. An application of theory and data will uncover Zephaniah's genre, as well as its main mode of presentation. When this process is complete a proper understanding of the book's literary nature is possible.

A Comparison of Zephaniah
to Epic and Lyric

As was stated in Chapter 2, an epic is a long poem that takes a single action or event for its subject and unveils that subject by a clear beginning, middle, and end. It is narrative in form, and able to tell about several events, however disparate, simultaneously. There is often a great number of stock phrases, ritual, elevated style, and universal themes in epic. Later epic describes catastrophic events, such as the origin of Rome in *The Aeneid* or the fall of the human race in *Paradise Lost*, in archetypal overtones. Narrators in epic tell why events happen, how characters feel, and what will happen in the future. Epics therefore seldom use dramatic narration.

There are very few similarities between Zephaniah and epic. While Zephaniah's scope is definitely universal, its subject, the day of Yahweh, is not described in nearly as much detail as the subject of a normal epic. Milton spends more space describing hell in *Paradise Lost* than exists in all of Zephaniah. Zephaniah has a distinct beginning, middle, and end, but presents these aspects in theological, not epic, terms. The day of Yahweh is an archetypal event akin to the fall of the human race in *Paradise Lost*. Redemption replaces destruction in Zephaniah, however, so it differs from the tragic ending of that epic. Zephaniah uses dramatic narration, thus differing from the constant third-person perspective in epic.

No real syntactical parallels between Zephaniah and epic can be drawn either. Except for the six 'says the Lord' passages, Zephaniah is not long enough for any series of stock phrases to arise. The prophecy is not highly stylized poetry, as is shown by its commentators. It is not ritualistic. Epic displays much more linguistic artifice than Zephaniah.

Characters in Zephaniah relate more to epic than any other aspect of the prophecy. As in the great epics there is a divine character in Zephaniah. Yahweh is not like classical gods, though, since He has no frailties such as jealousy, injustice, or impotence. Milton's God is much like Zephaniah's, but Milton molds his image of God with Christ in mind, an idea that is not apparent in Zephaniah. Even with the deity character, however, it is impossible to equate epic gods with Yahweh.

It is therefore obvious that Zephaniah is not an epic. Some parts of Zephaniah may seem vaguely epic, but there are not enough correspondences between the two to call Zephaniah epic prophecy. Too many thematic and linguistic likenesses are missing to make this connection.

Zephaniah is more compatible with lyric. Lyric is reflective, musical, self-contained, and ornamental (Frye, 1967:245). It is reflective in that it is addressed to God, an individual, or the poet. Lyric reflects personal feelings rather than a narrative plot, and normally extends no farther than its immediate topic. Characters may not even appear, since a certain mood is desired more than a depiction of realistic individuals. Because it is poetic, lyric features such ornamental devices as parallelism, meter, assonance, alliteration, similes, and metaphors.

Since it is composed in poetry Zephaniah displays many lyric linguistic devices. Alliteration is present in Zeph. 1.17-18, assonance in 3.1ff., and both similes and metaphors in 2.9. Metaphors for Yahweh include priest (1.7-8), judge (3.5, 8), and king (3.15). Metaphors for judgment include sweeping (1.2-3), cutting off (1.4), sacrifice (1.8), searching (1.12), darkness (1.15), battle (1.16), plunder (2.9), and purification (3.9). Parallelism is prevalent, as it is in the lyric poetry of the psalms. Synonymous parallelism, both simple (2.4) and complex (3.1ff.), appears, along with antithetic (1.13) and synthetic (1.14-16) parallelism. In short, Zephaniah displays most of the elements of Old Testament poetry. Mere poetic likenesses, however, are not significant enough to call Zephaniah lyric, since all Old Testament poetry shares common characteristics.

Despite certain linguistic affinities, Zephaniah differs from lyric in plot, characterization, scope, structure, and point of view. Zephaniah's plot, while less involved than epic, goes into much more detail than lyric. The prophecy has a well-developed conflict and resolution, which differs from most lyric. Yahweh and the prophet emerge as much fuller characters than the basically stereotypical characters in lyric. Few lyric poems feature characterization at all. Perhaps scope is the greatest point of divergence between Zephaniah and lyric. Lyric's scope is normally confined to the mind of the poet or at most to the poet and one other individual. Zephaniah has an international implied audience, a subject of universal scope, and a message that has an impact on all of creation. This observation is not made to place Zephaniah above lyric, since lyric's compact nature allows it personal insights not found in Zephaniah, just to note the difference between the two.

Lyric is different structurally than Zephaniah, and offers a divergent point of view. Dialogue orders the structure of the prophecy, while stages of inner contemplation create the framework for lyric. Lyric is usually narrated from a first- or third-person view. For instance, Psalm 23 is narrated in the first person, and Psalm 125 in the third person. Very little if any dramatized narration appears in lyric, particularly where two characters might be used. In short, Zephaniah's whole manner of presentation varies from lyric.

Quite obviously it is not possible to label Zephaniah lyric prophecy any more than to call the book epic prophecy. Despite sharing certain poetic techniques and imagery, the differences in plot, characterization, scope, structure, point of view, etc., indeed most of what makes up a literary work, are too many to ignore. Much about Zephaniah's poetic artistry can be gained from a study of poetry, but the book cannot be placed in the lyric genre.

This survey of Zephaniah's relationship to epic and lyric is, admittedly, quite brief. Earlier chapters of the book, however, prove the points made here. Further explanations can only bear out the obvious differences between Zephaniah, lyric, and epic.

A Comparison of Zephaniah to Drama

Because of the data gathered from the close reading of Zephaniah in
Chapter 3 it is possible to note many distinct parallels between
Zephaniah and drama. Each element of the prophecy explored
through close reading either has clear affinity with dramatic
elements or fails to differ greatly from drama. Thus, each aspect of
Zephaniah charted in Chapter 3 is now studied in the light of
similarities and differences with drama. Through this comparison a
clear decision regarding the dramatic nature of Zephaniah can be
made.

Structure and Dialogue

Dramatic structure can take many forms. At the most fundamental
level the framework of a drama is marked by scenes and acts, which
are basically major movements of the story. Scenes build upon one
another to form acts and the sum of these acts composes a play. Alan
S. Downer realizes the importance of the scene when he writes:

> The basic unit in the dramatic structure is properly called the
> *scene*; but it is necessary to be aware constantly that the term has
> several meanings in theatrical usage... As the basic unit of play
> construction, however, it means simply a portion of the total play
> in which the stage is occupied by an unchanging group of players
> (169-70).

Scenes end for various reasons, the chief of which is to move the plot
to a different point. Each scene adds something to the overall
presentation of the story. As Downer explains:

> Each of the scenes in the act is made up of varying amounts of
> three elements: exposition, action, and preparation. Exposition is
> the recounting of the past, action is the forward movement of the
> scene, and preparation is the hint of things to come, the
> unanswered question (170).

Every succeeding scene therefore is built upon previous action,
functions as a present plot device, and projects future plot
development.

Acts consist of scenes. Acts were originally divided in Greek drama
by the appearance of the chorus in the play. The chorus normally
appeared five times, creating five acts (Holman:7). Hugh Holman
notes that to 'varying degrees the five-act structure corresponded to
the five main divisions of dramatic action: exposition, complication,

climax, falling action, and resolution' (7). Since then the acts have coalesced so that most modern plays are three acts, with some plays even portraying only one act. From Holman's survey it is obvious that acts end at major points in the plot. One significant portion of the drama ends and another begins. Acts are not superfluous, or chosen at random, but are keys to how a drama must be understood.

Effective dialogue is critical in drama, since it is the playwright's main source of communication. Good dialogue illuminates plot, characterization, themes, and all other aspects of the play. Theodore W. Hatlen sets forth several standards for dialogue when he declares:

> Discourse in drama must be clear since the language must be immediately apprehended by the listener; in the theater, there is no turning back the page, no pause to weigh and consider a line before continuing to the next. The dialogue must be interesting despite the need for simplicity and economy. It should capture the spirit of life and character... The diction must be appropriate for the character and the situation. Lines do not exist in the theater as separate entities. They are always in context. They grow out of the emotionally charged incidents of the plot. The language of drama must be dynamic. As we have already suggested, speech is a form of action. The dialogue shows the character's relationship to others, reflects the progression of the action, indicates what is happening inside the characters, reveals their suffering, growth or decline. It is a means of articulating the clash of wills and the conflicting motivations (51-52).

Hatlen's statements cogently emphasize the importance of dialogue in drama. It is the major element the dramatist can use to unfold the various parts of his play. Dialogue's significance can hardly be overstated.

Zephaniah's structure parallels dramatic structure in a number of ways because it is constructed on a series of speeches. As in drama, the dialogue of Zephaniah reveals a plot, character, and themes. It moves the plot from one point to the next, always careful to hint at future events through skillful use of foreshadowing. Since the speeches in Zephaniah are arranged in pairs a sense of scenes emerges, and from the scenes grow an outline of acts.

Many scholars have noted the presence of three major parts of Zephaniah. S.R. Driver says these parts are destruction (chapter one), repentance (2.1-3.7), and restoration (3.8-20) (1891:341-42). Parts one and three of this scheme accurately reflect Zephaniah's emphasis, but part two over-emphasizes the role of repentance in restoration. The verse divisions are also incorrect. Childs' three portions are threats against Judah (1.2-2.3), threats against the nations (2.4-3.8), and promises to each (3.9-20) (458). Childs' three headings are basically correct, but like Driver he fails to divide the book according to the characters' speeches. While neither scholar mentions the superstructure of the book formed by the characters' speeches, both do notice the major divisions of Zephaniah. Three major divisions of the prophecy do exist, and they are fashioned by a series of provocative speeches.

The first major division of the book is 1.2-17. This section consists of five speeches, three by Yahweh and two by the prophet, that describe the general nature of the day of Yahweh. The first two speeches set forth the idea of catastrophic judgment and provide a name for that judgment. Speeches three and four state that Judah will suffer through the day of the Lord, and again state the nature of Yahweh's judgment. Yahweh concludes the first part of the prophecy by categorically saying that the sin of the people will result in condemnation (1.17).

Once a general notion of judgment is presented, the second major division of the book tells who will suffer with Judah in the great judgment (1.18-3.5). The prophet gives the first speech in this section, claiming that the 'shameful nation' Judah (2.1) will be joined in judgment by Philistia. Yahweh responds by adding Moab and Ammon to the list (2.8-10). The prophet agrees with God's destruction of their idols (2.11), only to be followed by Yahweh's condemnation of Cush (2.12). Finally, the prophet condemns Assyria and concludes his sober comments as he began them—with a denunciation of Judah (3.1-5). As in the first division, the speeches of the characters create the plot in the second section.

After the second division incredible tension exists. Judah and her neighbors are to be destroyed. A third division is needed to provide some relief to the reader. Yahweh's first speech offers hope through the day of Yahweh (3.6-13). A remnant will be saved that will be joined by nations purified by judgment. This development is foreshadowed in 2.3, 7, and 9. The prophet rejoices in this resolution (3.14-17), and is followed by the Lord's promises to the remnant.

One speech logically follows another, filling out or explaining what went before and moving ahead towards the end of the book.

As was stated in Chapter 3, it is the dialogue of Zephaniah that creates the prophecy's structure. The speeches in the book are recognizable by the constant shifting between first- and third-person speech. The reason the book cannot be divided at the places Driver and Childs suggest is that their schemes interrupt unfinished speeches. Dialogue moves the prophecy's story and establishes the personality traits of Yahweh and the prophet.

It is apparent that the structure and dialogue of Zephaniah reflect the same basic principles as in drama. Sets of speeches work together to form parts of the plot, thus serving as scenes. Groups of speeches that serve as scenes constitute a section of the plot, and therefore create acts. Three basic acts are evident in the text, the first (1.2-17) consisting of three scenes, the second (1.18–3.5) of three scenes, and the third (3.6-20) of two scenes. These scenes and acts fit well with basic dramatic plot theory, as is shown below.[1] Perhaps the most telling argument for the dramatic nature of Zephaniah's structure is its formation around sets of speeches. There is no doubt about the existence of these speeches grammatically or contextually, so their significance must be recognized. Zephaniah's structure and dialogue are therefore definitely dramatic.

Plot

Dramatic plot seeks to present the logical resolution of a major conflict or problem carefully established in the early part of the play. There are many ways to set up the conflict and many ways to resolve it, but without these two elements there is no basis for drama. Every part of the story must contribute to the plot. According to Aristotle:

> Now, according to our definition, Tragedy is an imitation of an action that is complete, and whole, and of a certain magnitude; for there may be a whole that is wanting in magnitude. A whole is that which has a beginning, a middle, and an end. A beginning is that which does not itself follow anything by casual necessity, but after which something naturally is or comes to be. An end, on the contrary, is that which itself naturally follows some other thing, either by necessity, or as a rule, but has nothing following it. A middle is that which follows something as some other thing follows it. A well-constructed plot, therefore, must neither begin nor end at haphazard, but conform to these principles (37-38).

All parts of the plot work together, resulting in a unified construction.

Five elements constitute a normal dramatic plot: exposition, complication, crisis, *denouement* (resolution), and falling action (Styan:71-74). Exposition introduces the situation of the play, complication is the combination of factors that precludes a simple resolution to the problem introduced in the exposition, crisis is the highest point of tension created by the *agon*, or conflict, *denouement* is the way the crisis is resolved, and falling action includes events that occur after the play's resolution (Hatlen:28-40). None of these five parts makes sense without the others. A logical connection exists between all five elements. Even with such an organic unity, though, conflict and resolution form the core of dramatic plot. Exposition exists to set up the conflict, complication to heighten it, and the crisis point to demand its resolution. Falling action provides an epilogue to the plot's resolution.

Zephaniah's plot follows dramatic principles. The logical progression of the speeches bears out this fact. Exposition occurs in the first two speeches (1.2-7), where the basic fact of the coming day of the Lord is established. All of creation is to be swept away, with no creature spared (1.2-3). Judah will share in the judgment, initially because of idolatry (1.4-7). The prophet's first speech (1.7) gives the day of sweeping a concrete designation—the day of Yahweh. Thus, the story's conflict is introduced in sketchy form. Yahweh will destroy the whole world, including Judah.

Verses 1.8-2.11 provide the plot's complication. Little by little the awesomeness and universality of God's judgment is unveiled, leaving little doubt about the seriousness of the Lord's intentions. In 1.8-13 Yahweh's speech particularizes the people's sin. They are syncretistic (1.8), violent and deceitful (1.9), lazy and blasphemous (1.12), and materialistic (1.13). Due to such sin the prophet's second speech warns Judah about the totality of the day of Yahweh (1.14-16), an idea seconded by Yahweh's final speech of the first act (1.17). The plot is complicated by more than Judah's sin, however, when the prophet begins a list of neighboring countries that will suffer through judgment with God's people. Philistia is named first (2.4-7), followed by Moab and Ammon (2.8-10), and Cush (2.12). What complicates the plot is that world-wide devastation is approaching not only because of Judah's sin, but because of the sins of every surrounding nation. Any resolution to the problem must also include these nations.

Another matter also provides plot complication. The prophet mentions a remant that can, possibly, escape the judgment in 2.3 and 2.7, and Yahweh acknowledges this remnant in 2.9. Possible salvation for other nations is also hinted at in 2.11. At this point some solution to the impending destruction of the whole world is proposed, but no avenue of resolution is offered. Tension has begun to build over how the strands of the plot will come together.

An extreme crisis point is reached in 2.13–3.5. Not only are relatively small nations like Moab and Ammon earmarked for destruction, but mighty countries like Assyria are as well (2.13-15).[2] No land, small or great, can survive the day of Yahweh. To heighten the tension, the prophet catalogues the sins of Jerusalem one more time (3.1-5) as if to make sure there is no mistake about their candidacy for annihilation. At this point the crisis is complete. There seems no way for Judah, her neighbors, or creation in general to survive the coming wrath of Yahweh. No mention is made of the remnant in this speech, which leads to the conclusion that all offers of salvation have been withdrawn.

At this point of extreme crisis Yahweh provides the plot's resolution (3.6-13). The day of the Lord will purify the remnant, and set it apart from its enemies. Yahweh also purifies the nations so they can worship Him (3.9). Again, it is the day of the Lord's purging impulse that forges this opportunity for Judah's enemies. It is ironic that the source of conflict is also the channel of resolution. This speech is the most pivotal in the whole prophecy, since it draws together all elements of the plot's exposition, complication, and crisis, and at the same time provides its resolution and begins the story's falling action. In two verses (3.8-9) the whole complexion of Zephaniah changes.

While falling action is initiated in 3.6-13, the final speeches by the prophet (3.14-17) and Yahweh (3.18-20) represent it most fully. After condemning Judah and the other nations the prophet is content to rejoice with the remnant, reassuring them that their deliverance is real. Yahweh expands His promise to the remnant in the book's concluding speech. No blessing is withheld from the remnant, just as no aspect of judgment was held back in 1.2-3. Despite great odds, Yahweh brings deliverance for a segment of His nation, thus providing the plot's *denouement*.

Clearly Zephaniah's plot conforms to dramatic plot principles. This similarity is based on more than plot elements common to all literature, since Zephaniah's resolution is swift like drama rather than detailed like narrative. The prophecy's length is not as great as most drama, but all the plot devices appear. As with structure and dialogue, the plot of Zephaniah best lends itself to the dramatic genre. Few if any significant variations from dramatic plot can be found in Zephaniah, which further strengthens the preceding arguments.

Characters and Characterization
Scholars use numerous titles for the characters in a play. Usually characters are categorized by how believable they are, the function they serve in the story, or how extensively the author presents their personalities. Lajos Egri thinks they should be characterized by how tridimensional they are. The three dimensions they must possess are physical, sociological, and psychological. Full, totally developed characters exhibit all three, while others possess these aspects in varying degrees (33-34). J.L. Styan, following traditional drama criticism, calls characters that display Egri's three criteria 'round' characters (68). These characters are realistic, and display a full range of human emotions, strengths, and frailties. 'Typed' characters lack some element of full characterization, and are normally stereotypical individuals. Such characters serve comedy best, where, for instance, a fool or villain is needed (Styan:68). 'Symbolic' characters are normally gods, angels, or archetypal figures like death, youth, etc., and therefore do not portray human experience (Styan:68). Finally, 'respresentative' characters are types of the human race such as the coward or hero (Styan:68). Each type of character fits into the play in important ways, moving the plot toward its ultimate resolution.

Characters react to one another differently in one kind of drama than in another. When Aeschylus added the second character to drama in Greek tragedy the two characters did not speak to one another as much as they provided information *for* one another (Kitto, 1950:55). Later the characters interacted more extensively with one another, always adapting to the type of drama being presented. In tragedy the hero reacts differently to the antagonist than in comedy, and the results of these reactions vary greatly. For instance, regardless of how vehemently he may fight his enemy, the tragic hero usually loses the physical or emotional war with the antagonist. Comic heroes, however, always overcome their foes, often including them in the victory. Every barrier to the hero's success is removed in comedy. No matter what type of drama is presented, then, the characters interact with one another in a way that advances the plot. Where this element is present good characters exist.

How the playwright practices characterization varies from epic and lyric. Theodore Hatlen rightly observes:

> Character may be delineated in four ways. First, character is delineated by appearance. The actor's physical qualities give an immediate stimulus to the audience.
> ... Second, character is revealed by speech. The kind of language employed by the person, his manner of speaking, his voice quality, his inflection pattern, pitch, rate, and general vitality, all say something about him.
> ... Third, character is established by action... Fourth, character may be revealed by what others say about him, and the way in which they react to him (43-46).

Any revelation of character in drama must be through sense impressions. Who and what they are must be seen or heard directly from the drama or its text. Authorial intrusion is seldom used to present or explain a character as it is in epic or lyric.

Zephaniah's characters correspond to dramatic characters in their development, interaction, and manner of presentation. As was shown in Chapter 3, Yahweh and the prophet are both characters that grow in personality as the prophecy proceeds. Yahweh's personality develops from a one-dimensional, wrathful God to a righteous, but merciful, deity. The prophet grows from only an interpreter of God's wrath to a sharer of revelation in his own right. Yahweh is presented as the purposeful, acting Lord of creation, while the prophet is portrayed as an insightful, obedient sharer of God's plans. Neither character merely mouths the ideas of the other, since both share original features of the book's presentation. Certainly Yahweh is the fuller of the two individuals, but both are 'round' characters.

The interaction between God and His prophet is one of the clearest parallels between Zephaniah and drama. Not once in the prophecy does Yahweh speak directly to the prophet or the prophet to Yahweh. Instead they respond to one another by providing plot elements the other uses in a subsequent speech. At the beginning of Zephaniah the prophet explains the name of judgment (1.7), and then explains the awesomeness of its fulfillment (1.14-16). Yahweh comments on the prophet's assertion that surrounding nations share

in the judgment with Israel (2.8-10, 12). The prophet reacts to
Yahweh's resolution to the plot in 3.14-17. Both characters are
dependent on the other to complete the play's plot and their own
characterization. In this way the plot and the characters become one,
thereby producing a unified literary piece. Because of this unity it is
unnecessary for the two to address one another, since the speeches
move the character without direct discourse. In fact, Zephaniah's
artistry is enhanced by this type of dialogue. Thus, it is the shifting
between characters in Zephaniah that produces the action. It is the
conflict and resolution caused by this alternating that links Zephaniah
to drama.

Because Zephaniah's characters are presented solely through
dialogue they are dramatic in nature. No third-person narrator
describes either character or tells what either is thinking. Without
the direct speeches of Yahweh and the prophet nothing would be
known about their personalities. Indeed, if the comments of either
character were missing the other's characterization would be
incomplete. Both individuals are characterized *only* by what one or
the other says and does. A closer link to dramatic presentation can
hardly be imagined.

Most aspects of dramatic characterization therefore appear in
Zephaniah. Yahweh and the prophet show character development,
interact with one another through dialogue, and are presented
through words and actions. They fit well with a dramatic plot. In the
three most important aspects of drama, then, structure, plot, and
characterization, Zephaniah is strikingly dramatic.

Themes
While themes are important to all genres, there are no specific
themes that are confined to any individual genre. All themes cross
generic lines. Themes concerning love, hate, judgment, and reconciliation appear in epic, lyric, and drama. Zephaniah's great theme,
the day of Yahweh and its consequences, could be presented
effectively in any of the three genres. It could be displayed in prose as
well as in poetry.

If any connection between Zephaniah's themes and those of drama
exists, it is in the fact that most dramas are constructed around a
unifying theme or motif. Tragedy's theme is often the downfall of a
god, person, or city. A great sense of loss is felt by the audience
because of this downfall. Comedy usually focuses on the overcoming

of obstacles, whether to love, peace, or whatever. Satire seeks themes that humble persons or institutions. Zephaniah's whole *mythos*, or story line, revolves around a view of the day of the Lord. This idea certainly holds the book together. Very little can be made of this fact, however, since epics and, particularly, lyric often have a central, unifying theme. A study of Zephaniah's theme does not greatly aid generic classification, though it is absolutely vital for a complete understanding of how themes complete and complement plot and characterization.

Point of View

Aristotle notes in *Poetics* three significant differences between genres: medium, object, and manner of imitation (23). 'Manner of imitation' means the point of view the writer employs. He declares:

> There is still a third difference—the manner in which each of these objects may be imitated. For the medium being the same, and the objects the same, the poet may imitate by narration—in which case he can either take another personality as Homer does, or speak in his own person, unchanged—or he may present all his characters as living and moving before us (33).

It is this final manner of presentation that 'the name of "drama" is given ... as representing action' (33). Drama's point of view differs from epic and lyric, then, through the playwright's willingness to allow the characters to tell the story. As Elder Olson summarizes:

> Conversely, a dramatic action is one which can be represented, directly or indirectly, by external behavior. Any kind of *physical* action can be represented directly; that is, by the actor's performing, in reality or seeming, the very act itself, such as putting on a kettle, kissing the heroine, and so on. By inner and private conditions— except when a character simply tells us what is going on inside him—can be set before us only indirectly; that is, through outward signs from which we can infer them ... in fact we see only the outward signs of these conditions (1966:19-20).

There can be no real argument that Zephaniah has a dramatic manner of presentation. Except for six occurrences of 'says the Lord' in the text, there is no hint of third-person narration outside the two main characters.[3] Even these six occurrences serve more as exclamation points than evidences of narration. What the reader learns about the day of Yahweh is revealed by the characters. What the reader discovers about either character is revealed by what that character says or does, or has said about him. The plot is fully revealed by the series of speeches that form the prophecy's structure, and all themes are introduced through characters instead of through a narrator.

Time

Drama has always completed its story within a short period of time. Because of this tendency Aristotle claims that drama

> has vividness of impression in reading as well as in representation. Moreover, the art attains its ends within narrower limits; for the concentrated effect is more pleasurable than one which is spread over a long time and so diluted. What, for example, would be the effect of the Oedipus of Sophocles, if it were cast into a form as the Iliad? (54-55).

Most often playwrights seek to present a 'concentrated effect' by confining their story to one day, or a few days.

Even when long periods of time are covered in drama telescoping devices are used to limit the length of presentation. One character may summarize the past in a single speech or series of speeches, thus informing the audience of the play's background. Several days may pass between scenes, but the dialogue of the characters reveals what has happened. The audience may be so familiar with the play's myth that no explanation of past events is necessary. Always, the length of the text offers the major clue to the *play's* length. Since the action must take place in one sitting, the best dramas choose a central event and fill in background material without obscuring that vital happening.

Yahweh's day of judgment is an imminent threat in Zephaniah. No time frame for its appearance is ever set. God simply bursts on the scene promising to destroy all He has created (1.2-6). The prophet likewise only says that the judgment will fall with great force (1.6, 14-16). Both characters leave the distinct impression that the day could come at any time. When repentance is mentioned it is as an urgent offer of the prophet (2.3). Mercy arrives with equal suddenness, purging Israel and her neighbors of all offending traits (3.8-9) and creating a new start for Judah (3.14-20). But again no time frame is offered.

What occurs in Zephaniah, then, is a concentrated presentation of mercy extended despite, and because of, God's judgment. This whole plot takes place in a few moments, and dwells on this one central idea. Zephaniah therefore aims at and achieves a vividness and concentration that grips the reader. The force and brevity of this presentation of the day of the Lord is equal to anything in the Old Testament. As John M.P. Smith states, 'No prophet has made the picture of the day of Yahweh more real' (176).

As with its structure, plot, characterization, and point of view, Zephaniah's concentrated time frame is dramatic. There is none of the extended story telling of narrative, but it is lengthy and involved enough to differ from lyric. Zephaniah chooses a single action for its plot, which corresponds to drama. It imitates the action in a compact, telescoped way, portraying in a few speeches the judgment of the whole world. To present a subject of such magnitude with such force in so small a space is a significant artistic achievement.

Of the three classical genres, Zephaniah quite obviously has the most affinity with drama. In fact, it displays so many characteristics of drama that it can be called dramatic in the generic, not modal, sense. Its characters, plot, time, structure, and point of view all lead to that designation, and its themes do not hinder this conclusion. Thus, if the methodology discussed in Chapters 1 and 2 is valid, then Zephaniah can legitimately be studied as drama.

Zephaniah as Prophetic Drama

In Chapter 2 a methodology for determining and understanding genre is proposed that stresses the division of literary works into genres. Epic, lyric, and drama are used as models, with classical distinctions for sub-genres and modes utilized as well. All of Chapter 3 and the previous sections of this chapter deal with the identification of genre, and firmly establish that within a classical framework Zephaniah takes a dramatic form. This section mentions genre and sub-genre, but deals particularly with Zephaniah's mode of present-ation. Of special concern is how Zephaniah's dramatic and prophetic characteristics mesh. To reveal this interrelationship it is necessary to reaffirm the book's dramatic nature, provide fuller definitions of 'mode', 'comic', and 'prophetic', and establish a synthesis of the classicist and biblical models. Without such a study the literary analysis of the book and Zephaniah's canonical context remain unnecessarily separate.

Without belaboring the point, it must be repeated here that a close reading of Zephaniah indicates it displays several traits of classical drama. It has a structure of alternating speeches between characters, a plot construction around a distinct conflict and resolution, a set of developing characters, and a dramatic point of view. Zephaniah also observes the three unities of drama: unity of place, unity of action, and unity of time. Its backdrop does not change throughout the play, as it does in a book like Ezekiel, Daniel, or Jeremiah. The action, or plot, is unified in its effort to show the purging and recreating nature of the day of Yahweh. Zephaniah's time frame is the eternal present. A sense of the imminent nature of the day of the Lord pervades the work. Thus, by all classical ways of defining drama Zephaniah is a drama.

Of course these dramatic elements are evident through a study of the book's text alone. Problems about date, staging, etc. may arise through historical studies. While such problems are far from insoluble,[4] they are not particularly relevant. The presence of closet drama, or literary drama, shows that all dramatic writing is not meant to be staged. What *is* important and relevant for this argument is that the written, literary, fixed, canonical text of Zephaniah reflects classical dramatic principles, and that it is only from the text that generic classification can be made.

Zephaniah eludes classical sub-genres identification. Aristotle sets forth two sub-genres of drama: tragedy and comedy (33ff.).

> Tragedy, then, is an imitation of an action that is serious, complete, and of a certain magnitude; in language embellished with each kind of artistic ornament, the several kinds being found in separate parts of the play; in the form of action, not of narrative; through pity and fear affecting the proper purgation of these emotions (36).

The reader or viewer of tragedy is supposed to 'thrill with horror and melt with pity at what takes place' (36). This audience reaction is elicited through the fall of a hero or heroine through some personal, cosmic, or societal flaw. The conclusion of a tragedy is fixed, and is often determined by unmovable fate.

Comedy, on the other hand, is

> an imitation of characters of a lower type—not, however, in the full sense of the word bad, the Ludicrous being merely a subdivision of the ugly. It consists in some defect or ugliness which is not painful or destructive. To take an obvious example, the comic mask is ugly and distorted, but does not imply pain (43).

As opposed to tragedy, comedy allows its hero or heroine to fend off all enemies and create a new utopian society. Since comedy ends amiably its conclusion is made more open ended than tragedy. Hope, not resignation, is the governing emotion at the end of comedy. Simply because comedy imitates 'lower' elements of life does not mean its message is trivial. Like tragedy its plot corresponds to life and creates a valuable mood in an audience. Concerning this mood Frye contends:

> We notice that just as there is a catharsis of pity and fear in tragedy, so there is a catharsis of the corresponding comic emotions, which are sympathy and ridicule, in Old Comedy. The comic hero will get his triumph whether what he has done is sensible or silly, honest or rascally (1967:43).

Therefore, two traditional sub-genres of drama exist. One portrays the fall of a character, the other the rise and exaltation of a character. One inspires fear, pity, and a completely closed ending, while the other moves the audience towards sympathy, hope, and an ending filled with possibilities. Neither totally fits Zephaniah. Zephaniah intends to instill fear and pity in its audience at times, but there is no fall of a tragic hero or pity-inspired ending. The book ends happily, but is not an imitation of the ludicrous. Its subject is a deadly serious one. It remains to be seen, then, how much further literary-critical models can illuminate Zephaniah.

Literary criticism makes a significant contribution to Zephaniah interpretation through its emphasis on mode. Northrop Frye says mode is:

> A conventional power of action assumed about the chief characters in fictional literature, or the corresponding attitude assumed by the poet toward his audience in thematic literature. Such modes tend to succeed one another in a historical sequence (1967: 366).

What Frye means when he speaks of the 'attitude(s) assumed' is that a mode is either the mood that prevails in a literary piece or a mixing of genres or sub-genres that facilitates a certain plot. Simply stated, 'mode' is the way genre and sub-genres are artistically portrayed. Particularly important for Zephaniah is the mixing of genres and sub-genres to achieve an effect, so this method of viewing mode is discussed below. Even if it has no definite sub-genre, the book does have a distinct mode.

Examples of the mixing method of mode are numerous. For instance, *The Iliad* is an epic that chronicles the death of Hector and fall of Troy through a tragic plot. *The Odyssey*, on the other hand, is an epic with a happy, comic ending. Within both there are also snatches of lyric and drama as well. Bits of genres and sub-genres within a work, however, cannot determine mode. Only an overriding use of a genre or sub-genre to achieve a specific 'attitude' qualifies as a definite mode. Thus, when the epic writer of *The Iliad* desires to create fear, pity, and a completely closed, apparently unjust ending in his work he uses a tragic mode to do so. Because *The Odyssey* recounts the triumphant home-coming of its hero comic modal devices dominate the story.

Since a definition of mode has been presented, it is necessary to suggest Zephaniah's mode. To do this, two terms are needed: comic and prophetic. The use of both terms helps to encompass the literary and canonical nature of the book and thereby fully to explain its mode. These terms also convincingly explain Zephaniah's dramatic-prophetic character. The two modes are defined with their synthesis in mind.

A comic mode employs the traits of comedy to forge a positive outlook for a work. Several elements occur in most comedy. They include:

1. The identification of the comic hero and the object of his desire
2. The coming of obstacles or enemies to defeat the hero
3. The triumph of the hero against all odds
4. The displaying of compassion or pity for the hero's enemies
5. The including of enemies in the hero's victory (Frye, 1967: 43-49)

One other characteristic is implicit in comic works, which is that the story serves as an example for its audience of how life can and should be. The last traits listed reveal that comic plots end with the hero successful and the possibility that even the hero's enemies can be forgiven and offered the spoils of the hero's victory. Struggles arise for the comic hero, but these problems are inexorably overcome. This favorable ending is what is meant by 'comic', not some humorous or ridiculous conclusion.

It is important to realize that a work need not display all five elements of comedy to have a comic mode. What is of importance is that difficulties are resolved and a conciliatory ending presented. Non-comic characters may have non-comic problems, but have them resolved through a comic ending. A comic mode therefore results. In short, the ludicrous side of comedy can be absent in a story cast in a comic mode.

Some brief elaboration of the five comic elements is necessary. The first trait indicates that early in a story the protagonist is identified, and this hero's aims and goals are presented. In Aristophanes' *Lysistrata*, Lysistrata is the heroine, and her goal is to end a long and unpopular war. Trait number two shows that opposition and obstacles to the hero's goal will arise. In fact, problems must come for the plot to develop. Lysistrata's main difficulty is that men love war and refuse to stop the fighting. Another obstacle is that once her plan to stop the war is suggested even some women oppose her. Both of these characteristics help establish the story's conflict. At this point in the plot it appears there is no help for the protagonist.

Each of the final three ideas helps provide the plot's resolution. No matter how severe the opposition to the comic hero becomes the hero will emerge victorious. Regardless of how many foes or problems arise the protagonist survives and triumphs. Lysistrata overcomes the opposition of the men and women in her society and brings an end to the war. Once the battle is won no grudge is held against the hero's enemies. Instead, compassion is felt for the enemy's plight. Because of this compassion, the enemy is invited to join the new idealistic society formed by the hero's victory. A model of this trait is when Lysistrata forgives her opponents and gives them a place in the newly peaceful society.

A more serious example of the inclusion principle is found in *The Merchant of Venice*. In Shakespeare's story Antonio borrows money from a Jewish moneylender named Shylock, promising a pound of his flesh if he is unable to pay. Shylock hates Antonio and intends to take the pound out of Antonio's heart. Antonio is unable to pay, but a court scene uncovers an obscure law that entitles Antonio to a pound of Shylock's flesh. Rather than exact that pound, however, Antonio forgives Shylock if he will become a Christian and pay a fine. Shylock is thereby allowed the privilege of becoming a full-fledged Venetian citizen. All is forgiven, albeit for a price. Northrop Frye comments on this inclusion theme:

> In Classical literature the theme of acceptance forms part of the stories of Hercules, Mercury, and other deities who had a probation to go through, and in Christian literature it is the theme of salvation, or, in a more concentrated form of assumption: the comedy that stands just at the end of Dante's *Commedia* (1967:43).

Various methods of defining 'prophetic' have appeared, with nearly all taking a historical approach. Because of the great emphasis on historical analysis there is a scarcity of material that addresses the literary nature of prophecy. A short survey of representative Old Testament introductions and books on prophecy proves this point. The following overview is brief, but includes the major movements in Old Testament studies of the past century.

Most scholars define 'prophecy' and 'prophetic' by charting the etymologies of Hebrew words translated 'prophet', by discussing the notion of prophecy held by Israel's neighbors, by speaking about the rise of 'classical prophecy' in the eighth century, by delineating the historical situations of pre-exilic and post-exilic prophets, and by debating the relationship between the prophets and the cult (Soggin: 211-40). Other writers stress the way prophets received and discharged their inspired message.[5] Still others discuss the role of the prophet among the political leaders of the day (Anderson: 231-32). Form critics designate individual pericopae and give them names, but always with historical situation and history of composition in mind. None of these studies deals exclusively with prophetic texts. While making a valuable contribution to a historical understanding of the prophets, these works do not describe what makes the prophets' *writing* 'prophetic'.

Childs presents the view mentioned above, but primarily attempts to explain why the written prophecies are included in the Old Testament canon (305-10). In doing so he tries to show how prophetic books fit into the canon with the law and writings. Instead of arriving at a comprehensive understanding of prophecy as a whole, however, Childs focuses on individual books. Even where he mentions collective prophecy he subordinates it to the forming of individual works (310). He also tends to discuss a canonical book in the light of how it spoke to its original audience. Despite centering on historical analysis, Childs also deals with the text and shape of books rather than just their background.

Von Rad's extensive and influential writings on the prophets blend historical and textual concerns. In *The Message of the Prophets* and volume two of *Old Testament Theology* he covers the historical ground charted by other scholars, citing the prophets' call, reception of revelation, and conception of God's word as major areas of study.[6] He also traces the origins of prophecy etymologically and canonically (1965: 6ff.). Besides these common historical concerns, von Rad discusses the manner in which the prophets received and transmitted oral and written traditions (1967:15-29; 1965:33-69). By attempting to understand the history of traditions von Rad points to the need to realize the words of prophecy have a history much as the prophets themselves have a history. He thus stresses that the text's message must be studied alongside historical concerns of the texts.

Two clear conclusions arise from this brief survey. First, historical critics deal with pre-textual matters. They want to know what happened *before* a text was written. Many advances have been made through their research, but absent from these advances is a better understanding of what makes a canonical text prophetic. A *text* is not prophetic because it reflects certain formulaic sayings, reveals cultic or political influence, was redacted for decades or centuries before reaching its final form, or calls its chief figure a 'seer' or 'prophet'. A text is prophetic because it shares ideas, themes, modes, or characteristics with other texts. Second, there is a great need for literary studies of canonical prophecy. More attention is needed on how the prophecies are alike and why they are placed together. In short, a sense of prophetic genre and mode must be attained. Parts of historical works, particularly those of von Rad and B.D. Napier, lean in those directions, but have to be reshaped to answer literary questions.

To arrive at a literary, modal definition of prophecy attention must center on canonical, written, fixed literature. Historical background should only enter the discussion when it directly affects the meaning of a text. More specifically, Zephaniah's prophetic nature ought to be defined as it relates to the book of the twelve's sense of prophecy, since canonically it has always been a part of that body of literature (Childs:309). The components of the twelve should be examined and Zephaniah's relationship to them noted. Therefore, an idea of prophetic literature and Zephaniah's place in it will emerge. Then the definition of prophetic should be compared to literary modes to fuse literary and biblical terms.

Various ideas are common to prophecy in general, and thus aid the search for a definition of prophecy. Though von Rad's work in historical studies is monumental, his most relevant contribution to this work is his recognition of common literary elements in the prophetic canon. He claims:

> Nevertheless, however bewildering the ease with which the prophets pass from one form of address to another, there are two constant factors which never fail to find a place with them all. The one is Yahweh's new work for Israel which he allowed the prophet to read off from the horizon of world-history. The other is the election tradition, within which the prophet and his hearers alike stand (1967:101).

Election does not bring security regardless of Israel's actions, though, since promises of judgment are mixed with assurances of election. As von Rad observes:

> The comfortable words of the tradition are, however, both called in question by the prophet's message of judgment and reconverted by him into an anti-typical new form of prediction. Thus, tensions created by three factors bring the prophet's *kerygma* into being. These are: the new eschatological word with which Yahweh addresses Israel, the old election tradition, and the personal situation, be it one which incurred penalty or one which needed comfort, of the people addressed by the prophet (1967:101).

These common factors are not presented identically in every prophet, but are present in some form in each (1967:101).

Thus, two elements, a new eschatological word for the prophet's day and the election of Israel, are located by von Rad in all the prophets. These two threads bind prophetic works together. The significance of von Rad's discovery is that these two strands are literary devices. When literary likenesses surface it is possible to discuss what constitutes literary prophecy, or prophetic genre. Beyond history, then, what von Rad views as prophetic is writing that includes these two aspects.

In a generally historical treatment of prophecy, B.D. Napier lists several ideas that comprise the content of prophecy (910-19). Napier agrees with von Rad that election is a recurring theme in prophetic writing, but correctly points out other dominant emphases. He thinks classical prophecy 'rises ... first in the consciousness that Israel now stands between Egypts, that what she was she will be again' (911). Israel was redeemed, sinned, judged, but will be redeemed again. A constant cycle exists in prophetic literature. To explain the cycle Napier notes seven common components of prophetic writing:

1. 'Thus says Yahweh': Word and symbol
2. 'Out of Egypt I called my son': Election and covenant
3. 'They went from me': Rebellion
4. 'They shall return to Egypt': Judgment
5. 'How can I give you up?': Compassion
6. 'I will return them to their homes': Redemption
7. A light to the nations: Consummation (910-19)

For Napier, the content of prophecy is a series of themes that composes an overarching Exodus motif. Napier makes a solid contribution to a literary definition of prophecy by showing what literary themes characterize prophetic books. These themes reveal the unified nature of prophecy, and have promise for discovering prophetic mode.

Since it is content that determines genre and mode, Napier's list is a good starting place for defining 'prophetic'. His seven items must be checked to see if they are present in the book of the twelve. The following list is a brief survey of where these themes appear in some of the eleven minor prophets and Zephaniah:

1. 'Thus says Yahweh': Word and symbol. 'Thus says Yahweh' appears in some form in every minor prophet except Habakkuk and Jonah. It appears six times in Zephaniah. Even in Habakkuk and Jonah the Lord speaks directly to the prophet.
2. 'Out of Egypt I called my son': Election and covenant. Hosea is the *locus classicus* for the election motif, but it is assumed in all the twelve. In Zeph. 2.8 Israel is called 'my people', which shows the special nature of Israel.
3. 'They went from me': Rebellion. No other element of prophecy is so common as the sinfulness of Israel and her neighbors. Obadiah, Jonah, and Nahum focus on the sins of the nations, while the other nine specifically mention Israel's iniquity. All nations are accountable for their sin. Zephaniah lists the transgressions of Israel (1.2–2.3; 3.1-5) and the nations (2.4-15).

4.   'They shall return to Egypt': Judgment. The logical result of sin is judgment in all the twelve. Judgment takes the form of the day of Yahweh in Joel, Amos, Obadiah, Zephaniah, and Malachi. It is the chief theme of Zephaniah.

5.   'How can I give you up?': Compassion. This impulse is most obvious in Hosea, but is also the driving force behind God's call to repentance. It is the motivation behind the restoration of Israel. In Zephaniah compassion is shown through Yahweh's choice of a remnant and the offer of hope to the nations.

6.   'I will return them to their homes': Redemption. With the possible exceptions of Habakkuk and Jonah, who do not speak extensively about *Israel's* sin, no matter how great the sin of Israel God promises to restore His people. Even the foreign nations will share in this restoration, as Jonah, Micah, and Zephaniah promise. Redemption extends, then, to the whole earth.

7.   A light to the nation: Consummation. Jonah exemplifies this theme. Napier is a bit redundant here, since Israel's witness to the nations is epitomized by the preceding motif.

Certainly other prevalent ideas could be mentioned. The remnant pattern quickly comes to mind. Still, Napier captures the essence of the literary elements that unite the book of the twelve. To say that these books are prophetic, therefore, is to say that they exhibit a sense of God's revelation, Israel's election, Israel's sin, God's judgment, God's compassion, and Israel's restoration. Each book relates these elements in a unique way because each has a creative author. Just as it is possible to know that a tragic work features the inevitable fall of a character in a closed, fated universe, so it is possible to say a book is prophetic because it contains these common elements.

Zephaniah is definitely prophetic in mode. Its whole plot revolves around common prophetic devices. Its conflict and resolution reflect its conformity with the other eleven minor prophets. Zephaniah shows the sin of God's people and the nations, the judgment of both through the day of Yahweh, God's compassion on them and the future blessings given them. Zephaniah displays the core of the prophetic mode.

In Chapter 3 of this work it was stated that Zephaniah's mode is comic, but in the preceding paragraph that the mode is prophetic.

Rather than a contradiction, however, these assertions are complementary. Notice how the characteristics of comic and prophetic literature fit together.

1. The identification of the comic hero and the object of his desire: the election of Israel. It is Yahweh who chooses Israel to be a special people for Himself and the nations to serve Him. Yahweh is the hero and Israel and her neighbors are the object of His desire.
2. The coming of obstacles or enemies to defeat the hero and frustrate his purpose: the rebellion of Israel and the sin of her neighbors. The sins recounted in 1.2–3.5 serve as the obstacles to Yahweh's purposes, and the scope of the day of judgment discourages hope.
3. The triumph of the hero against all odds: judgment of the whole earth. God's answer to His enemies is to completely devastate them. This judgment is the beginning of better things.
4. The displaying of compassion or pity for the hero's enemies: compassion for Israel and her neighbors. Zephaniah presents Yahweh's mercy through the choice of a remnant and the promise of the nations' coming to Him (2.11). God could destroy the whole human race, but chooses to spare some.
5. The including of enemies in the hero's victory: the redemption and restoration of Israel. In Zephaniah all enemies are allowed to share in the new society forged by the day of Yahweh. Just as Lysistrata and Antonio forgive their enemies, so the Lord redeems a portion of the earth's people.

The revelatory emphasis of prophetic writing is mostly absent in comic works, and, as stated above, Napier's seventh theme is misplaced. Otherwise the parallels between the prophetic and comic are obvious.

Since the prophetic and comic are so similar it is proper to conclude that Zephaniah has a comic-prophetic mode. It is just as correct, literarily speaking, to designate the book as either comic or prophetic. Biblical and literary terms are therefore able to illuminate one another. Through the interrelationship of these modes studies of comic and prophetic texts can be improved.

Summary

This chapter shows that in classicist terms Zephaniah is a drama. Every part of the book leads to this conclusion. Zephaniah's mode is prophetic-comic. Here both classicist and biblical terms agree. If it is possible to say a work is a comic drama, then it is also possible, given the right set of circumstances, to call a work a prophetic drama. This is the best description of Zephaniah, for it takes into account its literary and canonical characteristics.

Chapter 5

THE TEXT, OUTLINE, AND DIVISION OF ZEPHANIAH
AS A PROPHETIC DRAMA

The major task of this work is complete now that the genre and mode of Zephaniah have been established. This chapter serves as a summary to the project by offering a translation of Zephaniah, dividing the work into speeches, scenes, and acts, and providing textual notes for the translation.

The translation of Zephaniah follows some basic principles. First, the Biblica Hebraica Stuttgartensia (BHS) edition of the Masoretic text (MT) of the Old Testament is the basis for the translation. Other Hebrew editions exist, but BHS is considered the standard scholarly text. Second, the Hebrew is preferred over other versions, including the Septuagint (LXX). Certainly this decision is open to question. The LXX is older than the MT, but is a translation from Hebrew. Though relatively young, the MT is close to more ancient texts like the Dead Sea Scrolls. Third, changes in the MT are made only when the manuscript evidence for an emendation is overwhelming or when the alteration clearly offers the best translation. Fourth, since Zephaniah is poetry a conscious effort is made to reproduce its parallelistic phrases and metrical suggestions are offered. Perhaps the effort sometimes gives a verse an artificial sound. Still, the translation must reflect the writer's choice of linguistic genre even when the translator's choice of words is inadequate.

Divisions in the text are those suggested in Chapter 4. Speakers alternate when there are shifts between first- and third-person narration. The three acts follow the major movements of the book. Most scenes consist of a speech by each character, except when a soliloquy concludes an act. New sets of speeches almost always introduce a new plot element.

Textual notes comprise the last section of the chapter. Every note is set off by chapter and verse, is keyed to BHS, and is reflected in the translation. These notes are kept simple, with the hope that they are not simplistic. Every suggestion of BHS is mentioned, and other points relevant to Zephaniah as drama are covered.

Translation and Division of the Drama

1.1 Prose Prologue: The word of Yahweh which was to Zephaniah son of Cushi, the son of Gedaliah, the son of Amariah, the son of Hezekiah,[a] in the days of Josiah son of Amon, king of Israel.

Act One: 1.2-17

Scene One: General Judgment and Explanation

1.2	YAHWEH	I will sweep away[a] everything from the face of the earth, says Yahweh	3+3+2
1.3		I will sweep away[a] man and beast I will sweep away[a] the birds of the heavens and the fish of the seas.	3+3+2
		[b]I will overthrow[c] the wicked[b] and I will cut off man from the face of the earth, says Yahweh.	2+2+3+2
1.4		I will stretch out my hand against Judah and against all the inhabitants of Jerusalem.	3+3
		I will cut off [a]from this place[a] the remnant of Baal the[b] name of [c]the idolatrous priests,[c]	3+2+3
1.5		those who bow down on the roofs to the hosts of the heavens,	2+2
		those who bow down[a] swearing[b] to Yahweh[c] and yet who swear to Milcom,[d]	3+2
1.6		those who turn away from Yahweh and do not seek the Lord nor inquire of Him.	3+3+2

1.7	PROPHET	Be silent before the Lord God,
		   for the day of Yahweh is
		     near!
			4+4

		The Lord has prepared a sacrifice[a]
		   and has consecrated His
		     guests.
			3+2

		[a]On the day of Yahweh's sacrifice. . . .[a]	4

Scene Two: Judgment of Judah and Explanation

1.8	YAHWEH	I will punish the princes
		   and the sons[b] of the king
		     and all who dress
		       in foreign clothes
			2+2+2+2

1.9		[a]On that day[a] I will punish every-
		one
		   who leaps over the thres-
		   hold
		     who fills the house of
		     their Lords
		     with violence and deceit.
			3+3+3+2

1.10		It shall be [a]on that day[a] says
		Yahweh
		   a cry will come from the
		   Fish Gate
		     and howling from the
		     Second Quarter
		       and a loud crash from
		       the hills.
			4+4+2+3

1.11		Wail, inhabitants of the mortar,
		   for all the traders will be no
		   more;
			3+4

		all who are laden with silver will be cut off.	3+1

1.12		It shall be [a]at that time[a]
		I will search Jerusalem with a lamp[b]
		   and I will judge the men[c]
		   thickening on their lees,
			3+3+4

		who say in their hearts, 'The Lord will not do good, nor will He do evil.'	2+2+2

1.13		Their wealth will be plundered and their houses destroyed.	3+2
		[a]They will build houses, but not live in them.	2+2
		They will plant vineyards, but not drink wine from them.[a]	2+3
1.14	PROPHET	The great day of Yahweh is near, near and coming quickly.[a]	3+3
		[b]The sound of Yahweh's day is bitter, the mighty man cries out there.[b]	4+3
		That day is a day of wrath, a day of distress and trouble, a day of trouble and ruin,	4+3+3
		a day of darkness and gloom, a day of clouds and black- ness,	3+3
		a day of trumpet and battle cry, against the fortified city and against the high for- tifications.	3+3+3

Scene Three: Yahweh's Closing Soliloquy

1.17	YAHWEH	I will bring distress on mankind, and they will walk like the blind. [a]Because they have sinned against Yahweh,[a] their blood will be poured out like dust and their flesh[b] like dung.	2+2

Act Two: 1.18–3.5

Scene One: Soliloquy of Judgment and Hope

1.18	PROPHET	Neither their silver nor their gold will be able to save them.	2+2

[a]On the day of the Lord's wrath,   3+2+2
  in the fire of His jealousy,
    the whole earth shall be
     consumed,
for He will make a full and sudden   3+4
end
  to all the inhabitants of the
  earth.[a]

2.1-2   Gather yourself, O shameless nation,   5+3+3
  before the [a]decree comes forth,[a]
    before the [b]day passes
    over[b] like chaff,
[c]before the Lord's fierce anger comes   5+5
upon you
  before the day of God's wrath
  comes upon you.

2.3   Seek the Lord   2+2+3
  all you humble of the land[a]
    who do His commands.
Seek righteousness.   2+2
  Seek humility.
Perhaps you may be hidden   2+2
  on the day of God's wrath.

2.4   Gaza shall be abandoned   4+2
  and Ashkelon shall become a
  desolation.
Ashdod's people shall be driven out at   3+2
noon,
  and Ekron shall be up-
  rooted.

2.5   Woe to you inhabitants of the   4+2
Seacoast,
  O nation of the Cherethites.
[a]The word of Yahweh is   2+3
against you,[a]
  O Canaan,[b] [c]land of the
  Philistines,[c]
[c]I will destroy you,   1+2
  and none will be left.'

2.6   [b]The land by the sea,[b]   3+2
  where the Cherethites[c]
  dwell,

	will be[a] a place for shepherds and a pen for sheep.	1+2
2.7	[a]It shall become[a] the possession[b] of the remnant of the house of Judah.	2+3

	They[c] will find pasture there.
	They will lie down in the
	evening,
	    in the houses of Ash-
	    kelon,
		2+2+2

	For Yahweh their God will care for them. He will restore their fortunes.	4+2

Scene Two: More Judgment and Hope

2.8	YAHWEH	I have heard the taunts of Moab, and the insults of Ammon,	3+3

		who taunted my people
		    and made threats against their
		    borders.[a]
			3+2

2.9		Therefore as I live,
		    says Yahweh of hosts,[a]
		    the God of Israel,
			2+3+2

		Moab shall become like Sodom, and Ammon like Gomorrah––	3+3
		a place[b] of weeds and salt pits, a wasteland forever.	3+3

		The remnant of my people shall
		plunder them,
		    and the survivors of the nation
		    shall possess them
			3+3

2.10		[a]This shall be what they get for their
		pride,
		    because they insulted and mocked
		    the people of the Lord of hosts.
			4+6

2.11	PROPHET	[a]The Lord will be terrifying[b] to
		them,
		    for He will make lean[c] all the gods
		    of the land,
			3+5

		and every man in his place shall bow down to Him–– every region of the nations.	2+3

Scene Three: Final Threats

| 2.12 | YAHWEH | You also, O Ethiopians, | 2+3 |
| | | ^awill be slain by My sword.^a | |

2.12 YAHWEH   You also, O Ethiopians,   2+3
                ᵃwill be slain by My sword.ᵃ

2.13 PROPHET He will stretch out His hand against
                the North,
                    and He will destroy Assyria.
                He will make Nineveh desolate—   3+2
                dry as the desert.

2.14   Herds will lie down in her midst,   3+1
                    every beast of the earth;ᵃ
                even the pelican and the hedgehog   2+2
                    will lodge in her pillars.
                A voiceᵇ will echo through the   3+2+3
                windows,
                    desolationᶜ in the threshold,
                        ᵈfor her cedar works are laid
                        bare.ᵈ

2.15   This is the exultant city   3+2
                    that dwelt in safety,
                who said in her heart,   3+2
                    'I am and there is no other.'
                What a wasteland she has become—   3+2
                    a lair for wild beasts!
                Everyone who passes by her hisses.   4+2
                    He shakes his fist.

3.1   Woe to her who is rebellious and   3+2
                defiled,ᵃ
                    the oppressing city.

3.2   She listens to no voice.   3+3
                    She accepts no correction.
                She does not trust in Yahweh.   3+3
                    She does not draw near to her
                    God.

3.3   Her princes within her   2+2
                    are roaring lions.
                Her judges are ᵃeveningᵇ   3+3
                wolves
                    who leave nothingᵃ for the
                    morning.ᶜ

3.4   Her prophets are wanton,   2+2
                    treacherous men.
                Her priests profane the holy.   2+2
                    They do violence to the law.

[a]Yahweh is righteous in her midst;   3+3
He does no wrong.
Morning by morning   2+3
He brings His justice[b] to light.[c]
He does not fail,[b]   2+3
[d]but the unjust knows no shame.[d]

Act Three: 3.6-20

Scene One: Resolution

3.6	YAHWEH	I have cut off nations;	2+2
		their strongholds are in ruins.	
		I have laid waste their streets,	2+2
		with no one passing through.	
		Their cities are destroyed,	2+1+2
		[a]without a man,[a]	
		without an inhabitant.	
3.7		I said, 'Surely she will fear[a] me,	3+2
		she will accept[a] correction,	
		She will not lose sight[b] of all	3+2
		I have appointed against her!'	
		But they were still eager	3+2
		to make all their deeds corrupt.	
3.8		Therefore, wait[a] for me, says Yahweh,	3+3
		for the day I arise as a witness.[b]	
		For my decision is to gather nations,	4+2
		to assemble[c] kingdoms,	
		to pour out my wrath against them[d]—	3+3
		all my fierce anger;	
		[e]for in the fire of my jealous anger	3+2
		all the world shall be consumed.[e]	
3.9		Then I will purify the lips [a]of the peoples[a]	5+4+3
		[b]that all of them may call	
		on the name of Yahweh	
		to serve Him as one.[b]	
3.10		[a]From beyond the rivers of Ethiopia,	2+2+2
		[b]My worshipers, My scattered children,	
		shall bring My offering.	

3.11	[a]On that day[a] you shall not be ashamed	4+2+3
	of all your deeds	
	which you did to Me,	
	Because then I will remove from your	3+2
	midst those who exult in their pride,	
	and you will never again be haughty	3+2
	in my holy mountain.	
3.12	For I will leave in your midst a people,	3+2+3
	humble and lowly,	
	and they shall trust in Yahweh's name.	
3.13	[a]The remnant of Israel[a]	2+2
	shall do no wrong;	
	they will speak no lies,	2+2+2
	nor will a deceitful tongue	2+2+2
	be found in their mouths.	
3.14 PROPHET:	[a]Sing, O daughter of Zion!	2+2
	Shout, O Israel!	
	Rejoice and exult with all your heart,	3+2
	O daughter of Jerusalem!	
3.15	[a]The Lord has removed your punishment.[b]	3+2
	He has turned aside your enemies.[c]	
	The [d]King of Israel,[d] Yahweh, is in your midst,	4+3
	You shall never again fear[e] harm.	
3.16	[a]On that day, it shall be said to Jerusalem	4+2+2
	'Do not be afraid, O Zion,	
	do not let your hands fall limp!	
3.17	[a]Yahweh your God is in your midst[b]	3+2
	mighty to save.	
	He will exult over you with joy.	3+2
	[c]He will renew you in His love.[c]	
	He will rejoice over you with singing	3+2
	[a]As on the day of the appointed feasts.[a]	

Scene Two: Closing Soliloquy

3.18	YAHWEH	I will remove[b] from you[c] [d]the burden of reproach.[d]	3+3
3.19		[a]I will deal[b] with all your oppressors [c]at that time[c],	3+2
		and I will save the lame, and gather those I have scattered.	2+2
		I will give them praise and honor in every land where they were ashamed.[d]	3+2
3.20		[a]At that time I will bring you home.	4+3
		[b]At that time I will gather you.[b]	
		I will give you honor and praise among all the peoples of the earth	4+3
		when I restore your fortunes[c] before your eyes, says the Lord.	2+3

Summary of Dramatic Plot Elements

The following characteristics are traditional dramatic plot devices. They appear in Zephaniah in this order:

1. Exposition (1.1-7)
2. Complication (1.8–2.11)
3. Climax of Crisis (2.12–3.5)
4. Resolution of Crisis (3.6-13)
5. Falling Action and Conclusion (3.14–20)

Textual Notes on the Translation

1.1 (a) A few Syriac manuscripts read חלקיה ('Hilkiah') for חזקיה ('Hezekiah'). Without other significant manuscript evidence it is impossible to change the text.

1.2 (a) BHS proposes that אָסֹף אָסֵף ('I will sweep away') should read אָסֵף אֹסֵף thus making the second word a Qal active participle. This reading makes sense of a very obscure form (Hiphil?) and is the best choice. It must be admitted, however, that no textual evidence supports this change.

The first of six נאם יהוה sayings appears here. These are the only third-person narrations in the text.

1.3 (a) Cf. the comments on 1.2.

(b-b) The phrase והמכשלות את־הרשעים is absent in the LXX, but fits the verse's context, since 'I will overthrow the wicked' parallels 'I will cut off man from the face of the earth'.

(c) To achieve the above-mentioned meaning והמכשלות must be changed to והכשלתו as BHS notes.

The second 'says Yahweh' occurs in this verse.

1.4 (a-a) Because of the verse's meter BHS wants to remove מן־המקום הזה. Since it is impossible to know the poet's intention for the meter and there is no manuscript evidence for the deletion the phrase should stand.

(b) The LXX, Syriac, Targums, and Vulgate read ואת־שם ('and the name') instead of את־שם. This emendation is correct in view of the overwhelming manuscript evidence.

(c-c) The LXX does not have עם־הכהנים. In 1 Kgs 23.5 and Hos. 10.5 forms of הכמרים are assumed to mean 'pagan or idolatrous priests'. Here 'priests' is added, which could indicate a gloss. Beyond the LXX no manuscript deletes the phrase. Even if the form has an explanatory purpose it appears to be original with the Hebrew text and should remain.

1.5 (a) המשתחוים is missing in the LXX, probably because the initial use of the word was thought sufficient to convey the meaning 'the worshipers'. While a bit redundant the word does not hurt the verse's context.

(b) The editors of BHS think הנשבעים should be deleted. Cf. the preceding comments.

(c) The LXX reading Μελχου, which is supported by the Syriac and Targums, is not significantly different than במלכם. The problem arose in the transliteration of the word.

1.7 (a) In the LXX αυτου ('his') is appended to 'Yahweh's sacrifice' to create the possessive form.

1.8 (a-a) The phrase והיה ביום זבח יהוה ('and it shall be on the day of Yahweh's sacrifice') is considered an addition. BHS makes a similar judgment in 1.10. Apparently the editors believe most formulaic sayings of this nature are additions. No textual or contextual

evidence supports this claim, and it must rejected. This phrase ends
1.7 and leads into Yahweh's speech.

(b) In the LXX τον οικον is added to ועל־בני making 'and against the
sons of the house of the king'. Nothing is gained by this addition,
which seems to be a gloss by the LXX translators.

1.9 (a-a) Cf. comments on 1.8, a-a.

1.10 (a-a) Cf. comments on 1.8-9. The third occurrence of 'says
Yahweh' is in this verse.

1.12 (a-a) Cf. comments on 1.8-10.

(b) The LXX, Syriac, and Targums read בנרות ('candles') as
singular. These texts reflect the best sense of the verse.

(c) BHS suggests האנשים ('the men') should read השאננים ('the
arrogant'). Certainly the 'men' are 'arrogant', but that implication is
clear without a textual change.

1.13 (a-a) BHS proposes deleting the second half of the verse. A
reference is made to Amos 5.11 where a similar proverbial phrase
occurs. Once more the prejudice against formulaic sayings surfaces.
There is no reason to drop the sentences.

1.14 (a) BHS wants to change ומהר ('to hasten'), a Qal infinitive
construct, to וממהר ('hastening'), a Qal active participle. The
infinitive conveys the sense of a participle, but the fluid nature of the
infinitive construct allows for this meaning without altering the
text.

(b-b) The editors of BHS note a possible reading for קול יום יהוה מר
צרח שם גבור ('The sound of the day of Yahweh is bitter, the mighty
man cries out there'). This suggestion is interesting because of the
possible confusion of letters, but neither improves the context nor
has supporting manuscript evidence.

1.17 (a-) Despite the note in BHS, there is no strong reason to
believe this passage is an addition.

(b) The LXX, Syriac, and Vulgate read σαρκας ('flesh' for ולחמם
'bread'?). While the translation supports the LXX, לחם could have an
older meaning akin to 'flesh'.

1.18 (a-a) Cf. the comments on 1.17, a-a.

2.2 (a-a) BHS observes the difficulty of לדתחק ('birth of decree' or
'decree comes forth') and offers לא תרחקו ('not driven away'). While

the MT is obscure, the sense of the verse is intelligible and does not require emendation.

(b-b) עבר, 'passes over', is translated as a participle in the LXX. Either rendering expresses the intention of the tex.

(c-c) This phrase is lacking in some Hebrew manuscripts, probably because it is repeated in the next line. There is no strong reason to exclude the line, though, so it must remain. The repetition of the clause emphasizes God's anger.

2.3   (a) A few codices have ארץ ('earth') instead of הארץ ('the earth'), but the MT is the best reading.

2.5   (a-a) BHS believes דבר־יהוה עליכם ('the word of the Lord is against you') may be an addition to the text. The words serve the important function of introducing the quotation, 'I will destroy you, and none will be left'. The sentence is therefore vital to the verse and should not be removed.

(b) BHS proposes to delete ארץ פלשתים ('land of the Philistines') as a gloss of 'Canaan'. No manuscript lacks the two words, however, and such explanatory expressions are common in the Old Testament.

(c-c) BHS notes that 'land of the Philistines' could come after יושב, but nothing is gained by the change.

2.6   (a) One possible reading for והיתה is והית.

(b-b) חבל הים ('land by the sea') is not in the LXX, but does not harm the verse's context, so should remain.

(c) כרת ('Cherethites') is not in the Vulgate. No other manuscript agrees, so the MT is followed.

2.7   (a) BHS says the whole verse is probably an addition to the original text. No doubt it is called late because it mentions the remnant and contains promises akin to 3.14–20. No textual evidence supports this conjecture.

(b) The LXX adds της θαλασσης ('by the sea') to חבל to match 2.6. This reading reflects the desire for clarity more than a textual variation.

(c) BHS thinks עליהם ('to them') should be על־הים ('by the sea'). While there is no manuscript evidence for the suggestion it is a much better contextual reading.

2.8   (a) The LXX has τα ορια μου ('my border') for על־גבולם ('their border'), but one LXX manuscript is the same as the MT. While the

LXX translation agrees with 'my people' there is no overwhelming reason to prefer it over the MT, since the MT fits the verse's context.

2.9 (a) צבאות ('hosts') is absent in the LXX. In a formulaic expression like 'says the Lord of hosts' it is not strange for 'hosts' to be left out of a translation. Either reading leaves the verse's meaning intact. This is the fourth third-person passage in the book.

(b) BHS notes מורש ('expression') could replace ממשק ('possession').

2.10 (a) BHS states this verse may be an explanatory preface to 2.11 and thus an addition to the text. The verse is in all major manuscripts, fits the context of 2.8, and concludes the first-person speech begun in 2.8-9. It therefore plays a significant role in this, Yahweh's fourth, speech.

2.11 (a) This verse is also called a probable addition. It starts the fourth prophetic speech, fitting the context as a matching speech for 2.12. These short speeches serve as pausal devices in the plot.

(b) The LXX and Syriac read επιθανησεται ('he shall appear') for נורא ('he will be terrifying'), so BHS says the best reading may be נראה ('he shall appear'). Perhaps the emendation is in order, but the sense of the verse in either proposal is that Yahweh comes with frightening force against Moab and Ammon. For Him to appear is terrifying.

(c) BHS suggests רזה ('he destroys') could be ירזה the imperfect form of the word. No manuscript evidence supports a variant reading, though, and the MT communicates the intention of the verse.

2.12 (a-a) This verse's ending is extremely difficult. BHS states that some words may be missing after המה. No other manuscripts shed significant light on the verse. Though BHS is probably correct, the MT is the only available version.

2.14 (a) The LXX has της γης ('the earth') for גוי ('nation') which is a good change. While גוי could refer to 'all the nations' the Greek translation is clearer.

(b) BHS exchanges כום ('owl') for קול ('voice'). No manuscript supports the proposal, and previous mentions of birds in the verse sufficiently convey the source of the sounds.

(c) The LXX has κόρακες ('ravens') for חרב ('desolation'). Since ערב means 'raven' BHS thinks that word could replace 'desolation'.

Thus, 'an owl will echo through the windows, a raven through the threshold'. If the emendation of 2.14b is accepted the LXX is the best text, but if not the MT is correct. It is more plausible that the LXX confuses an *ayin* for a *heth* than the MT confusing קול and כוס, so the MT is followed.

(d-d) This phrase is declared corrupt and deleted by BHS. Though difficult, there is no manuscript evidence for its removal.

3.1 (a) BHS observes that ומאלה ('defiled') could actually be ('treacherous') because of the closeness in sound of *aleph* and *ayin*. The MT is probably correct, but both words imply Jerusalem's sinfulness.

3.3 (a) BHS concludes that this sentence could read לא עזבו גרם זאבים ('Her judges are wolves that leave no bone until morning'). BHS's idea required too many parallels between dissimilar words and letters to be accepted.

(b) The LXX reads της Αραβίας ('the desert') for ערב ('evening'), thus making 'desert wolves' of 'evening wolves'. The presence of לבקר ('until morning') supports the MT.

(c) There is no need to delete 'until morning'. Cf. 3.3b.

3.5 (a) BHS wonders if this verse is an addition. It fits the context of the prophet's speech and no manuscript omits it.

(b-b) The LXX omits לאור לא נעדר ('He does not fail'), but other versions include the expression. The phrase contrasts the goodness of Yahweh and the shame of Israel. Since it fits the context it should remain.

(c) Because of the Syriac and Aramaic translations of לאור it is possible the preposition could be כ. No shift in meaning results from this variant reading.

(d-d) BHS notes a variant Greek translation of this phrase. The LXX has και ουκ εις νικος αδικιαν. εν διαφθορα ('and injustice shall not prevail. Because of corruption I will cut off the nations'.) This translation shows God's victory over sin, but does not contrast the sin of human beings and the righteousness of Yahweh. Without other manuscript support the MT should not be altered.

3.6 (a-a) Cf. 1.4, a-a.

3.7 (a) BHS proposes תיראי (second feminine singular—'you will fear me') be changed to the third-person feminine singular form ('she will fear me'). The LXX, Syriac, and Aramaic versions make the word a second plural. No manuscript follows BHS, but their suggestion makes the form coincide with עליה and reflects the verb's feminine characteristics, so it is followed in the translation.

(b) Both the LXX and Syriac read 'her sight(instead of 'her dwelling'. Therefore מעונה should be מעיניה. This alteration fits the context of Yahweh's correction of the city better than the MT.

3.8   (a) The LXX and Vulgate translate חכו as singular, which makes better grammatical sense.

(b) Instead of לעד ('for prey' or 'plunder') the LXX and Syriac have εις μαρτυριον ('to witness'). Thus God rises 'to witness' against rather than 'to plunder' the nations. The Greek and Syriac versions fit the judicial scene of the nations' gathering very well, and is followed in the translation.

(c) The first person singular possessive ending is left out of לקבצי in the Cairo Codex, but is present in all major manuscripts.

(d) BHS says the more probable suffix for עליהם is כם. No justification for the change exists, though, so the MT should stand.

(e-e) BHS believes this threat is an addition, but it fits the immediate context and the spirit of the book as a whole. This is the fifth verse that includes a third-person passage.

3.9   (a-a) Some of the Judean Desert 11 (1969) manuscripts change אל־עמים to עלהעמים. Either maintains the text's meaning, but all other versions support the MT.

(b-b) BHS concludes that this phrase is an addition and also thinks the whole verse may be a gloss. Perhaps BHS calls the verse late because it stresses the nations' salvation. This salvation is, however, an indisposable part of Zephaniah's plot, as was seen in Chapter 3. No manuscripts support the idea that the verse is late.

3.10   (a) Cf. 3.19, b-b.

(b-b) Though as BHS claims עתרי בת־פוצי is absent in the LXX, the Greek specifically says Yahweh is to receive sacrifices from beyond Ethiopia, which implies that scattered servants of Yahweh will bring those sacrifices. The context indicates, then, that the MT is correct.

3.11 (a-a) BHS deletes ביום ההוא because of the verse's meter. Again, the poet's intention for his meter in unknown, no manuscripts omit the words, and the context does not warrant the change.

3.13 (a-a) BHS observes that 3.12b and 3.13 are metrically connected.

3.14 (a) As have many other commentators, BHS conjectures that 3.14–20 is an addition. Since this ending caps the entire drama, and indeed is foreshadowed throughout the book, to remove these verses would destroy the purpose of every part of Zephaniah.

3.15 (a) Cf. 3.14, a.

(b) The Targums point מִשְׁפָּטַיִךְ as מִשְׁפָּטִיךְ, which does not alter the word's meaning.

(c) The LXX, Syriac, and Aramaic point איבך ('your enemies') as איבך. Again the meaning does not change.

(d-d) The Luciani recension of the LXX reads βασιλευσει ('he will reign'). In this scheme מלך changes to ימלך. The major LXX texts read βασιλευς, however, which supports the MT. No emendation is necessary without stronger manuscript evidence.

(e) The LXX preserves οφη ('you will not see') rather than תיראי ('you will not fear'). The Syriac supports the Greek translation. Either conveys the idea that Israel's problems will disappear. The MT's is probably the best reading because of the verse's context and the ease with which the LXX and Syriac could have misread the Hebrew.

3.16 (a) Cf. 3.14, a.

3.17 (a) Cf. 3.14, a.

(b) The Leningrad Codex puts the *shewa* in the final *kaph*, which is the best pointing.

(c-c) BHS suggests יחריש ('He will quiet') should be יחרש ('He will renew') to follow the LXX and Syriac. The verse's context favors 'renew' because 'quiet' is out of character with the loud rejoicing of the rest of 3.17. It is also possible a *daleth* was changed to a *resh*.

3.18 (a-a) the LXX places 'as on a festival day' at the end of 3.17 and begins 3.18 with 'I will remove'. This is the clearest reading, is probably metrically correct, and makes sense of the rest of the verse. It must be said, though, that any translation of this verse is open to question.

(b) Cf. 3.14, a.

(c) The LXX suggests that ממך could possibly read מכם, thus transposing two letters. No advantage is gained by this switch.

(d-d) BHS correctly declares חיו corrupt, and suggests with the LXX that הוי ('woe') is the proper reading. Nothing else makes sense of the word.

3.19   (a) Cf. 3.18, b.

(b) The Targums add כלה after עשה making the text say 'I will make an end of your oppressors'. No other major manuscripts agree with the Aramaic, so the MT is followed.

(c-c) Cf. comments on 1.8-10.

(d) An alternate reading of the ending of the verse is to insert 'when I restore their fortunes'. The removal of shame fits the renewal themes of 3.19 and reflects the return of exiles from the ends of the earth, so the MT is probably accurate.

3.20   (a) Cf. 3.18, b.

(b-b) BHS suggests changing קבצי to אקבץ, which creates a clearer syntactical sequence for this phrase, but has no manuscript evidence for support. Also, קבצי and בשובי are companion forms in the verse, thus showing consistency in the MT.

(c) In the LXX, Syriac, Vulgate, and medieval Hebrew manuscripts שבותיכם reads שבותכם. There is no reason to ignore the unanimity of these significant manuscripts, so the MT ought to be emended. The final third-person saying occurs in this verse.

NOTES

Notes to Chapter 1

1. *Ibid.*, p. 342. Driver noted that Wellhausen denied the authenticity of 2.8-11 and believed ch. 3 is also an addition to the text, Budde rejected 2.4-15 as incongruent with ch. 1, and Kuenen found 3.14-20 post-exilic in origin.

Notes to Chapter 2

1. Note the formalists' emphasis on knowing a stanza's form as a key to understanding its meaning. Cf. Cleanth Brooks and Robert Penn Warren, *Understanding Poetry* (4th edn; New York: Holt Rinehart and Winston, 1976), pp. 493-574.

2. In Chapter 3 of this book some of these features are explored to discover Zephaniah's genre.

3. Also note Kitto's discussion of justice in *The Oresteia* in Kitto, *Greek Tragedy*, pp. 98-99.

Notes to Chapter 3

1. It must be said at this point that every shift between first- and third-person speech is treated as a speech except for Yahweh's brief threat in 2.5. This promise—'I will destroy you, and none will be left'—is a quotation of Yahweh by the prophet.

2. This viewpoint is opposed to Moulton's assertion that 'the structure . . . is entirely in the Doom form'. Cf. Moulton, *The Literary Study*, p. 124.

3. Cf. Amos 1.13-2.3.

4. Cf. 1.2, 3(3), 4(2), 8, 9, 12, 17; 2.5, 8, 9; 3.6(2), 7, 8(2), 9, 11, 12, 18, 19(3), 20(4).

5. Cf. 2.12, 3.7, 8(3), 10(2), 11.

6. Cf. 3.8, 10, 11.

7. An explanation of the role of Zephaniah's characters in narration is offered later in this section.

8. All of these passages have the traditional Hebrew words נאם־יהוה except for 2.9, where the phrase is expanded to 'declares the Lord of hosts, the God of Israel', and 3.20 where אמר יהוה is used.

Notes to Chapter 4

1. Chapter 5 divides the text into scenes and acts to show how the prophecy reads as a drama.

2. For a clear understanding of Assyria's power during the reign of Josiah consult John M.P. Smith, *Zephaniah*, pp. 159-71.

3. The six passages are 1.2, 3, 10; 2.9; 3.8, and 3.20.

4. For instance, Kapelrud suggested that the prophet may have presented this book to the nation at the feast of ingathering and that his message may be influenced by dramatic presentations of enthronement psalms. Cf. Kapelrud, *Zephaniah*, p. 51. If Kapelrud is correct, a specific time for Zephaniah's staging is plausible.

5. Cf. R.K. Harrison, *Introduction to the Old Testament* (Grand Rapids: Eerdmans, 1983), pp. 751-59, and E.J. Young, *My Servants the Prophets* (Grand Rapids: Eerdmans, 1974).

6. Gerhard von Rad, *The Message of the Prophets*, trans. D.M.G. Stalker (New York: Harper and Row, 1967), and Gerhard von Rad, *Old Testament Theology: Vol. Two*, trans. D.M.G. Stalker (New York: Harper and Row, 1965). While this brief sketch of von Rad's work in no way does justice to his contributions to Old Testament studies, it does mark the major movements of his work on prophecy.

BIBLIOGRAPHY

1. Books: Historical-Critical

Anderson, Bernhard, W. *Understanding the Old Testament*. 3rd edn; Englewood Cliffs, N.J.: Prentice-Hall, 1975.

Calvin, John. *Commentary on the Twelve Minor Prophets: Habakkuk, Zephaniah, Haggai*. Trans. John Owen, 1848; rpt. Grand Rapids: Eerdmans, 1950.

Childs, Brevard. *Introduction to the Old Testament as Scripture*. Philadelphia: Fortress, 1980.

De Souza, Bernard. *The Coming of the Lord*. Jerusalem: Franciscan Press, 1970.

Driver, S.R. *An Introduction to the Literature of the Old Testament*. 1891; rpt. Gloucester, Mass.: Peter Smith, 1972.

—*The Minor Prophets Nahum, Habakkuk, Zephaniah, Haggai, Zechariah, Malachi: Introductions, Revised Version with Notes, Index, and Map*. Edinburgh: T.C. and E. Jack, 1906.

Eakins, Frank. 'Zephaniah', *Broadman Bible Commentary*. Vol. 7. Nashville: Broadman, 1973.

Elliger, Karl. *Das Buch der Zwölf Kleinen Propheten*. Vol. 2. Göttingen: Vandenhoeck & Ruprecht, 1950.

Francisco, Clyde T. *Introducing the Old Testament*. Rev. edn; Nashville: Broadman, 1977.

Harrison, R.K. *Introduction to the Old Testament*. Grand Rapids: Eerdmans, 1969.

Irsigler, Hubert. *Gottesgericht und Yahwetag*. St Ottilien: Eos, 1977.

Kapelrud, Arvid S. *The Message of the Prophet Zephaniah*. Olso-Bergen-Tromso: Universitätforlaget, 1975.

Keil, C.F. *The Minor Prophets*. Trans. James Martin. Commentary on the Old Testament, Vol. 10; 1869: rpt. Grand Rapids: Eerdmans, 1980.

Kelley, Page H. *Micah, Nahum, Habakkuk, Zephaniah, Haggai, Malachi*. The Layman's Bible Commentary, Vol. 14. Nashville: Broadman, 1984.

Krinetzki, Günter. *Zefanjastudien: Motiv- und Traditionskritik + Kompositions- und Redaktionskritik*. Frankfurt: Peter Lang, 1977.

Lambert, W.G. *Babylonian Wisdom Literature*. London: Oxford University Press, 1960.

Luther, Martin. *Lectures on the Minor Prophets*, Trans. Richard J. Dinda. Luther's Works, Vol. 18. St. Louis: Concordia, 1975.

Mowinckel, Sigmund. *The Psalms in Israel's Worship*. Vol. 1. Trans. D.R. Ap-Thomas. Nashville: Abingdon, 1979.

von Rad, Gerhard. *The Message of the Prophets*. Trans. D.M.G. Stalker. New York: Harper and Row, 1967.

—*Old Testament Theology*. Vol. 2. Trans. D.M.G. Stalker. New York: Harper and Row, 1965.

Sabottka, Liudger. *Zephaniah: Versuch einer Neuübersetzung mit philologischem Kommentar*. Rome: Biblical Institute Press, 1972.

Smith, George Adam. *The Book of the Twelve Prophets*. Vol. 2. Garden City, N.Y.: Doubleday, Doran and Co., 1929.

Smith, John M.P., William H. Ward, and Julius A. Bewer. *A Critical and Exegetical Commentary on Micah, Zephaniah, Nahum, Habakkuk, Obadiah and Joel*. The

International Critical Commentary. New York: Scribner's, 1911.

Smith, Ralph. *Micah-Malachi*. Word Biblical Commentary, Vol. 32. Waco: Word, 1984.

Soggin, J. Alberto. *Introduction to the Old Testament*. Rev. edn. Trans. John Bowden. Philadelphia: Westminster, 1980.

Stonehouse, G.G.V. *The Books of the Prophets Zephaniah and Nahum*. The Westminster Commentary. London: Methuen, 1929.

Watts, John D.W. *The Books of Joel, Obadiah, Jonah, Nahum, Habakkuk, and Zephaniah*. The Cambridge Bible Commentary. London: Cambridge University Press, 1975.

Young, E.J. *My Servants the Prophets*. Grand Rapids: Eerdmans, 1974.

2. Books: Literary-Critical

Allen, Gay Wilson and Harry H. Clark. *Literary Criticism: Pope to Croce*. Detroit: Wayne State University Press, 1962.

Alter, Robert. *The Art of Biblical Narrative*. New York: Basic Books, 1981.

—*The Art of Biblical Poetry*. New York: Basic Books, 1985.

Aristotle. *Poetics*. Trans. S.H. Butcher in *Dramatic Theory and Criticism: Greeks to Grotowski*. Ed. Bernard F. Dukore. New York: Holt, Rinehart and Winston, 1974.

Berlin, Adele. *Poetics and Interpretation of Biblical Narrative*. Sheffield: Almond Press, 1983.

Bieber, Margarete. *The History of the Greek and Roman Theater*. 2nd edn; Princeton, N.J.: Princeton University Press, 1971.

Booth, Wayne C. *A Rhetoric of Irony*. Chicago: University of Chicago Press, 1974.

—*The Rhetoric of Fiction*. Chicago: University of Chicago Press, 1963.

Brooks, Cleanth and Robert Penn Warren. *Understanding Poetry*. 4th edn; New York: Holt, Rinehart and Winston, 1976.

Bush, Douglas. *English Literature in the Earlier Seventeenth Century: 1600-1660*. 2nd edn; New York: Oxford University Press, 1962.

Colie, Rosalie. *The Resources of Kind: Genre-Theory in the Renaissance*. Ed. Barbara Lewalski. Los Angeles: University of California Press, 1973.

Crane, R.S. ed. *Critics and Criticism: Ancient and Modern*. Chicago: University of Chicago Press, 1952.

Croce, Benedetto. *Aesthetics*. Trans. Douglas Ainslie. New York: Noonday Press, 1968.

Culpepper, R. Alan. *Anatomy of the Fourth Gospel: A Study in Literary Design*. Philadelphia: Fortress, 1983.

Dace, Wallace. *Elements of Dramatic Structure*. Manhatten, Ks.: Ag Press, 1972.

Downer, Alan S. *The Art of the Play: An Anthology of Nine Plays*. New York: Henry Holt, 1955.

Dubrow, Heather. *Genre*. London: Methuen, 1982.

Egri, Lajos. *The Art of Dramatic Writing: Its Basis in the Creative Interpretation of Human Motives*. Boston: The Writer, 1960.

Eliot, T.S. *Selected Essays*. New York: Harcourt Brace, 1950.

Esslin, Martin. *An Anatomy of Drama*. New York: Hill and Wang, 1977.

Fergusson, Francis. *The Idea of a Theater*. Princeton, N.J.: Princeton University Press, 1949.

Forster, E.M. *Aspects of the Novel*. New York: Harcourt Brace Jovanovich, 1955.

Fowler, Alastair. *Kinds of Literature*. Cambridge, Mass.: Harvard University Press, 1982.

Frye, Northrop. *Anatomy of Criticism*. New York: Atheneum, 1967.

—*The Great Code: The Bible and Literature*. New York: Harcourt Brace Jovanovich, 1982.

Gerhart, Mary and Allan M. Russell. *Metaphoric Process: The Creation of Scientific and Religious Understanding*. Fort Worth: Texas Christian University Press, 1984.

Gilbert, Allan H. *Literary Criticism: Plato to Dryden*. Detroit: Wayne State University Press, 1962.

Good, Edwin M. *Irony in the Old Testament*. 2nd edn; Sheffield: Almond Press, 1981.

Guerin, Wilfred L., *et al. A Handbook of Critical Approaches to Literature*. New York: Harper and Row, 1966.

Hanford, James H. *A Milton Handbook*. 4th edn; New York: Appleton-Century-Crofts, 1954.

Hatlen, Theodore W. *Orientation to the Theater*. New York: Appleton-Century-Crofts, 1962.

Holman, C. Hugh. *A Handbook to Literature*. 3rd edn; New York: Odyssey Press, 1972.

Kitto, H.D.F. *Form and Meaning in Drama*. London: Methuen, 1960.

—*Greek Tragedy*. 2nd edn; Garden City, N.Y.: Doubleday, 1950.

—*Poiesis: Structure and Thought*. Los Angeles: University of California Press, 1966.

Kugel, James. *The Idea of Biblical Poetry*. New Haven, Conn.: Yale University Press, 1981.

Lewis, C.S. *A Preface to Paradise Lost*. London: Oxford University Press, 1959.

Lowth, Robert. *Lectures on the Sacred Poetry of the Hebrews*. Trans. G. Gregory. Andover: Codman Press, 1829.

Moulton, Richard G. *The Literary Study of the Bible*. Rev. edn; Boston: Heath, 1899.

Olson, Elder. *The Theory of Comedy*. Bloomington, Ind.: Indiana University Press, 1968.

—*Tragedy and the Theory of Drama*. Detroit: Wayne State University Press, 1972.

Plato. *Dialogues*. Trans. S.H. Butcher. *Dramatic Theory and Criticism: Greeks to Grotowski*. Ed. Bernard F. Dukore. New York: Holt, Rinehart and Winston, 1974.

Preminger, Alex, O.B. Hardison, Jr, and Kevin Kerrane. *Classical and Medieval Literary Criticism: Translations and Interpretations*. New York: Ungar, 1974.

Roberts, Edgar V. *Writing Themes about Literature*. 3rd edn; Englewood Cliffs, N.J.: Prentice-Hall, 1973.

Robertson, David. *The Old Testament and the Literary Critic*. Philadelphia: Fortress, 1977.

Rogers, William Elford. *The Three Genres and the Interpretation of Lyric*. Princeton, N.J.: Princeton University Press, 1983.

Rose, H.J. *A Handbook of Greek Literature*. 4th edn; London: Methuen, 1950.

Scott, Wilbur. *Five Approaches to Literary Criticism*. New York: Collier, 1962.

Strelka, Joseph P. *Theories of Literary Genre*. University Park, Penn.: Pennsylvania University Press, 1978.

Styan, J.L. *The Dramatic Experience*. London: Cambridge University Press, 1965.

Wellek, Rene and Austin Warren. *Theory of Literature*. New York: Harcourt, Brace, 1949.

Wimsatt, William K. and Cleanth Brooks. *Literary Criticism: A Short History*. New York: Alfred A. Knopf, 1967.

3. Periodicals: Historical-Critical Articles

De Roche, Michael. 'Zephaniah I 2-3 "The Sweeping" of Creation'. *Vetus Testamentum* 30 (1980), 104-109.

Fensham, F.C. 'The Book of Zephaniah'. *The Interpreter's Dictionary of the Bible: Supplementary Volume*. Nashville: Abingdon, 1976.

Ferguson, H. 'The Historical Testimony of the Prophet Zephaniah'. *Journal of Biblical Literature* (1883), 42-59.

Gerstenberger, E. 'The Woe-Oracles of the Prophets'. *Journal of Biblical Literature* 81 (1962), 249-63.

Gray, John. 'A Metaphor from Building in Zephaniah II 1'. *Vetus Testamentum* 3 (1953), 404-407.

Hyatt, J. Phillip. 'The Date and Background of Zephaniah'. *Journal of Biblical Literature* 68 (1949), 25-29.

Jeppesen, Knud. 'Zephaniah I 5-6'. *Vetus Testamentum* 31 (1981), 372-73.

Leslie, E.A. 'Zephaniah, Book of'. *The Interpreter's Dictionary of the Bible: R-Z*. Nashville: Abingdon, 1962, 951-53.

Rice, Gene. 'The African Roots of the Prophet Zephaniah'. *The Journal of Religious Thought* 36 (1979), 21-31.

Smith, Louise and Ernest R. Lacheman. 'The Authorship of the Book of Zephaniah'. *Journal of Near Eastern Studies* 9 (1950), 137-42.

Williams, Donald. 'The Date of Zephaniah'. *Journal of Biblical Literature* 82 (1963), 77-88.

4. Periodicals: Literary-Critical Articles

Barr, James. 'Reading the Bible as Literature'. *Bulletin of the John Rylands University Library* 56 (1973), 10-33.

Clines, David J.A. 'Story and Poem: The Old Testament as Literature and as Scripture'. *Interpretation* 34 (1980), 115-27.

Coleridge, Samuel Taylor. 'Biographia Literaria', *Anthology of Romanticism*. 3rd edn. Ed. Ernest Bernbaum. New York: Ronald Press, 1948, 331-73.

Crane, R.S. 'English Neoclassical Criticism: An Outline Sketch'. *Critics and Criticism: Ancient and Modern*. Ed. R.S. Crane. Chicago: University of Chicago Press, 1952, 372-88.

Gerhart, Mary. 'Generic Studies: Their Renewed Importance in Religious and Literary Interpetation'. *JAAR* 45 (1977), 309-25.

Gottwald, Norman K. 'Poetry, Hebrew'. *Interpreter's Dictionary of the Bible: K-Q*. Nashville: Abingdon, 1962.

Hazlitt, William. 'On Familiar Style'. *Anthology of Romanticism*. 3rd edn. Ed. Ernest Bernbaum. New York: Ronald Press, 1948, 405-407.

Keast, W.R. 'The Theoretical Foundations of Johnson's Criticism'. *Critics and Criticism: Ancient and Modern*. Ed. R.S. Crane. Chicago: University of Chicago Press, 1952, 389-407.

Milton, John. 'The Reason of Church Government Urged Against Prelaty'. *The Portable Milton*. Ed. Douglas Bush. New York: Viking Press, 1968, 123-30.

Muilenburg, James. 'Form Criticism and Beyond'. *Journal of Biblical Literature* 88 (1969), 1-18.

Napier, B.D. 'Prophet'. *Interpreter's Dictionary of the Bible: K-Q*. Nashville: Abingdon, 1962, 896-919.

Nations, Archie L. 'Historical Criticism and the Current Methodological Crisis'. *Scottish Journal of Theology* 36, 59-71.

Robertson, David. 'Literature, The Bible As'. *Interpreter's Dictionary of the Bible: Supplementary Volume*. Nashville: Abingdon, 1976, 547-51.

Ryken, Leland. 'Literary Criticism of the Bible: Some Fallacies', *Literary Interpretations of Biblical Narratives*. Ed. Kenneth Gros Louis, James S. Ackerman, and Thayer S. Warshaw. Nashville: Abingdon, 1974, 24-40.

Wordsworth, William. 'Preface to the Second Edition of "Lyrical Ballads"'. *Anthology of Romanticism*. 3rd edn. Ed. Ernest Bernbaum. New York: Ronald Press, 1948, 300-10.

5. *Dissertations: Historical-Critical*

Edens, Ambrose. 'A Study of the Book of Zephaniah: As to the Date, Extent and Significance of the Genuine Writings, with a Translation'. Ph.D. dissertation, Vanderbilt University, 1954.

Williams, Donald Leigh. 'Zephaniah: A Re-Interpretation'. Ph.D. dissertation, Duke University, 1961.

6. *Dissertations: Literary-Critical*

Ball, Ivan Jay Jr. 'A Rhetorical Study of Zephaniah'. Th.D. dissertation, Graduate Theological Union, 1972.

INDEX

INDEX OF BIBLICAL REFERENCES

INDEX OF AUTHORS

JOURNAL FOR THE STUDY OF THE OLD TESTAMENT

Supplement Series

* Out of print